# Scalable AI and Design Patterns

## Design, Develop, and Deploy Scalable AI Solutions

Abhishek Mishra

*Scalable AI and Design Patterns: Design, Develop, and Deploy Scalable AI Solutions*

Abhishek Mishra
Mumbai, Maharashtra, India

ISBN-13 (pbk): 979-8-8688-0157-0               ISBN-13 (electronic): 979-8-8688-0158-7
https://doi.org/10.1007/979-8-8688-0158-7

Managing Director, Apress Media LLC: Welmoed Spahr
Acquisitions Editor: Celestin Suresh John
Development Editor: Laura Berendson
Coordinating Editor: Gryffin Winkler

Cover designed by eStudioCalamar

Cover image by rawpixel.com on freepik (www.freepik.com)

Distributed to the book trade worldwide by Apress Media, LLC, 1 New York Plaza, New York, NY 10004, U.S.A. Phone 1-800-SPRINGER, fax (201) 348-4505, e-mail orders-ny@springer-sbm.com, or visit www.springeronline.com. Apress Media, LLC is a California LLC and the sole member (owner) is Springer Science + Business Media Finance Inc (SSBM Finance Inc). SSBM Finance Inc is a **Delaware** corporation.

For information on translations, please e-mail booktranslations@springernature.com; for reprint, paperback, or audio rights, please e-mail bookpermissions@springernature.com.

Apress titles may be purchased in bulk for academic, corporate, or promotional use. eBook versions and licenses are also available for most titles. For more information, reference our Print and eBook Bulk Sales web page at http://www.apress.com/bulk-sales.

Any source code or other supplementary material referenced by the author in this book is available to readers on GitHub (https://github.com/Apress). For more detailed information, please visit https://www.apress.com/gp/services/source-code.

Paper in this product is recyclable

# Table of Contents

# About the Author

**Abhishek Mishra** is a seasoned data science and analytics professional with extensive expertise in information technology services and products. With a remarkable 15-year track record, Abhishek has leveraged his data science knowledge and engineering skills to analyze vast datasets, interpret findings, and communicate actionable insights to drive effective business decision-making. He has successfully led global analytics teams, developed cutting-edge machine learning solutions, and formulated data analytics strategies for esteemed organizations like Marsh McLennan, Fiserv India Pvt Ltd, and Deloitte Inc.

# About the Technical Reviewer

**Krishnendu Dasgupta** is currently the Head of Machine Learning at Mondosano GmbH, leading data science initiatives focused on clinical trial recommendations and advanced patient health profiling through disease and drug data. Prior to this role, he cofounded DOCONVID AI, a startup that leveraged applied AI and medical imaging to detect lung abnormalities and neurological disorders.

With a strong background in computer science engineering, Krishnendu has more than a decade of experience in developing solutions and platforms using applied machine learning. His professional trajectory includes key positions at prestigious organizations such as NTT DATA, PwC, and Thoucentric.

Krishnendu's primary research interests include applied AI for graph machine learning, medical imaging, and decentralized privacy-preserving machine learning in healthcare. He also had the opportunity to participate in the esteemed Entrepreneurship and Innovation Bootcamp at the Massachusetts Institute of Technology, cohort of the 2018 batch.

Beyond his professional endeavors, Krishnendu actively dedicates his time to research, collaborating with various research NGOs and universities worldwide. His focus is on applied AI and ML.

# Introduction

Welcome to the exploration of scalable AI systems—a journey through the intricacies of building intelligent solutions that stand resilient in the face of evolving demands and challenges. In this book, we embark on a comprehensive exploration of scalable artificial intelligence, unraveling the core concepts, techniques, and considerations that underpin the development of robust and adaptable intelligent systems.

## Who This Book Is For

This book is designed for a broad audience ranging from aspiring data scientists and AI enthusiasts to seasoned professionals and decision-makers seeking a deeper understanding of scalable AI. Whether you are a developer aiming to enhance your skills, a data engineer navigating the complexities of scalable data processing, or a business leader looking to harness the potential of intelligent systems, this book provides insights tailored to diverse roles and expertise levels.

## Structure of the Book

Our journey unfolds across twelve chapters, each dedicated to a critical aspect of scalable AI systems. We begin with a foundational understanding in Chapter 1, gradually progressing through the intricacies of scalability, data engineering, algorithms, infrastructure, deployment, real-time applications, edge computing, governance, and ethics. The book culminates in a forward-looking Chapter 11, where we explore future trends and emerging technologies shaping the landscape of scalable AI. Finally, Chapter 12 provides a holistic conclusion, offering key takeaways, emphasizing the importance of scalable AI, and reflecting on the design patterns crucial for building robust intelligent systems.

# Overview of Chapters

Chapter 1: Introduction to Scalable AI Systems

This chapter sets the stage by providing an overview of scalable AI systems, elucidating their significance, and highlighting the pivotal role of design patterns in constructing robust intelligent solutions. We delve into the challenges and considerations that shape the landscape of scalable AI.

Chapter 2: Fundamentals of Scalability in AI

Our journey deepens as we explore the fundamentals of scalability in AI. From handling large datasets to parallel processing techniques, this chapter lays the groundwork for understanding the core concepts essential for scalable intelligent systems.

Chapter 3: Data Engineering for Scalable AI

Data engineering practices take center stage in Chapter 3, addressing the critical role of data ingestion, preprocessing, feature engineering, and strategic data storage in supporting scalable AI systems.

Chapter 4: Scalable AI Algorithms and Models

In this chapter, we venture into the realm of algorithms and models tailored for scalability. Distributed training techniques, online learning approaches, and model parallelism take precedence as we examine their role in handling large-scale data and computing requirements.

Chapter 5: Scalable AI Infrastructure and Architecture

The foundation of scalable AI is intricately linked to infrastructure and architecture considerations. Containerization, orchestration, resource management, and auto-scaling strategies come under the spotlight as we explore their significance in building scalable AI systems.

Chapter 6: Scalable AI Deployment and Productionization

The journey progresses to the deployment and productionization aspects of scalable AI systems. We delve into model versioning, deployment strategies, monitoring, and performance optimization, providing insights into building production-grade AI systems.

Chapter 7: Scalable AI for Real-Time and Streaming Data

Addressing the dynamic demands of real-time and streaming data scenarios, Chapter 7 explores the challenges and techniques for implementing scalable AI in high-velocity, real-time applications and inference.

Chapter 8: Scalable AI for Edge Computing

Chapter 8 navigates the unique considerations of applying scalable AI in edge computing environments. From edge device architectures to model optimization and edge-to-cloud integration, we unravel the intricacies of extending scalability to the edge.

Chapter 9: Scalable AI Governance and Ethics

Ethical considerations take the forefront in Chapter 9, where we explore the governance and ethical dimensions of developing and deploying scalable AI systems. Bias mitigation, interpretability, and privacy considerations are pivotal components of this exploration.

Chapter 10: Case Studies and Best Practices

Bringing theory into practice, Chapter 10 presents real-world case studies and best practices, offering tangible insights into the successful implementation of scalable AI solutions. It serves as a guide for designing and implementing scalable AI systems effectively.

Chapter 11: Future Trends and Emerging Technologies

As we peer into the future, Chapter 11 delves into the emerging trends and technologies that will shape the field of scalable AI. From advancements in cloud computing to the integration of edge computing and cutting-edge AI hardware innovations, we explore the next frontier of intelligent systems.

Chapter 12: Conclusion and Final Thoughts

Our journey concludes with Chapter 12, where we distill key takeaways from the book, emphasize the enduring importance of scalable AI, and offer final reflections on the design patterns crucial for building robust intelligent systems.

# Embark on the Journey

The world of scalable AI systems awaits your exploration. Whether you are a novice eager to grasp the fundamentals or a seasoned professional seeking insights into emerging trends, this book is crafted to be your companion on this intellectual voyage. Let us delve into the intricacies of scalable AI, unlocking the potential to create intelligent systems that stand resilient in the face of evolving challenges and contribute to the transformative landscape of artificial intelligence.

# CHAPTER 1

# Introduction to Scalable AI Systems

Artificial intelligence (AI) is rapidly altering many facets of our lives, from personalized suggestions on streaming platforms to self-driving cars traversing crowded streets. Scalability in AI systems is becoming increasingly important as AI applications get more complicated and prevalent. In this chapter, we will delve into the topic of scalable AI systems, learning what they mean and why they are essential, as well as exploring an overview of various scalable AI system architectures with real-world examples.

## Understanding Scalability in AI Systems

Scalability refers to a system's capacity to handle a growing workload efficiently while maintaining performance. Scalability in the context of AI systems refers to the ability of systems to handle rising amounts of data, increasing computational requirements, and expanding user expectations without experiencing delays or crashes. Consider a well-known online shopping platform during a sale event.

If the platform's AI-driven recommendation system cannot handle the unexpected increase in users, the system may slow down or even crash, resulting in dissatisfied customers and lost business possibilities.

Example: Netflix's scalable recommendation system

Netflix, a popular streaming service, employs AI to recommend movies and shows to its users.

As the user base grows and more content is added, the recommendation system needs to handle an ever-increasing dataset. A scalable AI system ensures that even during peak usage times, users receive personalized recommendations without experiencing delays.

© Abhishek Mishra 2024
A. Mishra, *Scalable AI and Design Patterns*, https://doi.org/10.1007/979-8-8688-0158-7_1

# Why Scalability Matters in AI

Why Scalability Matters in AI

Handling Big Data          Meeting User Demand

Business Expansion          Cost effectiveness

complicated algorithms

**Handling Big Data**: For training and decision-making, AI systems rely on massive volumes of data. As the volume of data increases, the system must process and analyze it more efficiently. Scalable AI systems can handle enormous datasets without sacrificing performance.

**Meeting User Demand**: AI-powered applications such as virtual assistants or language translation tools must answer quickly, regardless of the number of users accessing the service at the same time. Scalability guarantees that user requests are handled as soon as possible.

**Business Expansion**: Scalable AI systems enable business expansion. For example, an ecommerce platform should be able to handle higher traffic during sales or promotions without degrading customer experience.

**Cost-Effectiveness**: Non-scalable systems may have periodic hardware upgrades to stay up with demand. Scalable designs can disperse workload over existing resources, eliminating the need for frequent hardware updates.

**Deep Learning Models and Algorithms**: Deep learning models and complicated algorithms necessitate substantial computational resources. Scalable solutions are required to distribute computing effectively as AI models grow larger and more complex.

Scalability is the foundation upon which strong and adaptive AI systems are constructed. We hope to provide a full grasp of these features and their practical ramifications as we travel through numerous dimensions of scalability, such as performance, vertical, data, model, operational, platform, and hybrid scalability.

1. **Performance Scalability**

    The ability of an AI system to handle increased workloads while retaining optimal performance is referred to as performance scalability. This is especially important in cases when the volume of data or the complexity of computations increases. A scalable AI system should be able to smoothly expand its capabilities to meet increased demand without sacrificing responsiveness.

    Example:

    Consider an ecommerce platform using AI for personalized recommendations. As the number of users and products increases, the AI system must scale its performance to deliver timely and relevant recommendations, ensuring a smooth user experience even during peak traffic.

2. **Vertical Scalability**

    Vertical scalability is the process of improving the capabilities of a single computer resource, usually by increasing its power, capacity, or efficiency. This is frequently accomplished by hardware upgrades, such as the addition of more powerful processors, increased memory, or enhanced GPU capabilities.

    Example:

    In a vertical scalability scenario, a machine learning model that initially ran on a single processor with limited memory may be upgraded to a more powerful server with multiple processors and significantly larger memory. This allows the model to handle larger datasets and complex computations more efficiently.

3. **Data Scalability**

   Data scalability refers to a system's ability to handle increasing data quantities. This comprises efficient data storage, retrieval, and processing systems that can scale to larger datasets without sacrificing performance or reliability.

   Example:

   A social media platform implementing scalable AI must efficiently manage and analyze the expanding user-generated content. Data scalability ensures that the platform can process and derive insights from an ever-growing pool of posts, images, and interactions.

4. **Model Scalability**

   Model scalability is concerned with the ability of machine learning models to adapt to changing and diversified requirements. A scalable AI model should be able to adapt to changes in data patterns, address new use cases, and integrate seamlessly with evolving infrastructures.

   Example:

   A predictive maintenance model deployed in an industrial setting needs to be scalable to accommodate new sensor data, handle variations in machinery, and adapt to different maintenance requirements as the industrial environment evolves.

5. **Operational Scalability**

   The efficient administration and deployment of AI systems as they expand in size and complexity are what operational scalability entails. This involves system administration, monitoring, and maintenance considerations to enable smooth operations at scale.

   Example:

   In a cloud-based AI service, operational scalability ensures that the system can handle an increasing number of user requests, automatically allocate resources as needed, and maintain reliable performance even during periods of high demand.

6. **Platform Scalability**

The scalability of platforms extends beyond individual systems to include the entire AI ecosystem. It entails a scalable AI platform's capacity to support the integration of various tools, frameworks, and technologies to fulfill the varying needs of users and applications.

Example:

A healthcare organization adopting a scalable AI platform must be able to seamlessly integrate different medical imaging analysis tools, electronic health record systems, and AI algorithms to create a comprehensive and interoperable AI ecosystem.

7. **Hybrid Scalability**

To provide the best performance and flexibility, hybrid scalability integrates various scalability methodologies. This could include a mix of vertical and horizontal scalability, on-premises and cloud-based solutions, or the integration of various AI models and algorithms.

Example:

A financial institution implementing a hybrid cloud solution for fraud detection may use vertical scalability for resource-intensive tasks like deep learning model training while employing horizontal scalability for handling real-time transaction data across distributed cloud servers.

# Key Considerations for Scalable AI Systems

- **Load Balancing**: Distributing incoming requests evenly across multiple resources prevents overloading one machine while others are underutilized.

- **Data Partitioning**: Dividing datasets into smaller subsets for processing by different machines ensures efficient data handling.

- **Fault Tolerance**: Building redundancy into the system ensures that if one component fails, the system can still function without interruption.

- **Auto-Scaling**: Implementing mechanisms that automatically add or remove resources based on demand prevents performance bottlenecks.

- **Data Consistency**: When multiple instances of an application are running, ensuring data consistency across all the cases is essential for accurate results.

# The Need for Design Patterns in Scalable AI

As the adoption of artificial intelligence (AI) systems grows, the necessity for scalability in AI designs becomes critical. Scalable AI systems allow for the effective management of growing datasets, increasing processing loads, and increasing user interactions. Design patterns are well-established solutions to typical issues that arise during software development.

Design patterns are critical in striking a balance between performance, resource utilization, and maintainability in the context of scalable AI systems. Let's look at why design patterns are important:

1. **Modularity and Reliability**

   A modular approach to system design is encouraged by design patterns. It is easier to comprehend, manage, and extend complicated AI systems by splitting them down into smaller, independent components.

   Because separate components can be scaled independently, this modularity also enables scalability.

   The "Observer Pattern" is a behavioral design pattern that specifies a one-to-many dependency between items so that when one object (the subject) changes its state, all of its dependents (observers) are immediately notified and updated. In a nutshell, the Observer Pattern creates a mechanism for a subject to notify many observers of any changes in its state, providing a loose coupling between the subject and its observers.

Using the "Observer Pattern" to alert different components about user preferences in a recommendation system, for example, ensures that any recommendation algorithm may be modified or replaced without affecting the entire system.

2.  **Adaptability and Flexibility**

    AI systems must frequently adapt to new requirements, data sources, and user behavior. Design patterns give the system flexibility by separating issues and allowing it to change without severe disturbances.

    For instance, the "Strategy Pattern" enables an AI system to dynamically transition between multiple algorithms or models, adapting changes in the underlying data distribution or user preferences.

    The Strategy Pattern is a behavioral design pattern that describes a family of algorithms, encapsulates each one, and allows them to be interchanged. It allows a client to select an appropriate algorithm at runtime, allowing the client to change its behavior without modifying its structure.

3.  **Resource Administration**

    Scalability requires effective resource management. Design patterns can help optimize resource utilization by offering rules on how components should interact and allocate resources, whether they be CPU, memory, or storage.

    The Factory Pattern is a creational design pattern that provides an interface for creating objects in a superclass while allowing subclasses to change the type of objects created. It belongs to the class of creational design patterns, which are concerned with the process of object creation in software development.

In layman's terms, the Factory Pattern is used to build objects without defining the specific class of the object. Instead of explicitly invoking a constructor to build an object, a factory method is utilized. This method is defined in an interface or abstract class, and its subclasses implement it.

The "Factory Pattern" can be used to produce and maintain AI model instances, for example. This guarantees that models are efficiently instantiated, eliminating resource wastage.

4. **Parallelism and Concurrency**

To meet user requests, scalable AI systems frequently need to do many tasks concurrently. Concurrency and parallelism design patterns aid in the efficient management of these tasks.

The Thread Pool Pattern is a concurrency design pattern used in software development to manage and control the execution of numerous threads within a program. In this approach, a pool of pre-initialized worker threads is generated and maintained, ready to execute tasks concurrently. Instead of creating a new thread for each job, the application delegates tasks to the current pool of threads, enabling effective resource utilization and lowering the overhead associated with thread creation.

For instance, the "Thread Pool Pattern" can be used to handle concurrent requests for AI services. It limits the number of threads that can execute concurrently, reducing resource exhaustion.

# Challenges and Considerations in Scalable AI Systems

While design patterns might be helpful, constructing scalable AI systems is not without difficulties. Let us look at some of the major issues and considerations:

1. **Data Volume and Speed**

   Managing massive amounts of data streaming in real time can be challenging. Scalable AI systems must be able to efficiently consume, process, and store data while maintaining performance.

   Consideration: Using data partitioning techniques like sharding or stream processing to assist in dividing data processing work across several resources

2. **Model Complexity**

   As AI models become increasingly complex, they necessitate enormous computational resources. Scalable AI systems must ensure that these resource-intensive models are distributed and managed efficiently.

   Consideration: Using containerization technologies like Docker and Kubernetes to distribute model training and inference workloads across containers and computers

   The Docker documentation provides comprehensive information on using Docker for different applications, including machine learning. The official documentation can be found here: `https://docs.docker.com/reference/`.

   The official Kubernetes documentation offers extensive information on deploying and managing applications, including those related to machine learning. The documentation is available here: `https://kubernetes.io/docs/home/`.

3. **Responsiveness and Latency**

   AI-powered apps, such as virtual assistants or real-time analytics platforms, must respond quickly even when under tremendous stress.

   Consideration: Allocating requests to the most accessible resources and caching frequently requested data, load balancing, and caching methods can minimize response times.

4. **Redundancy and Fault Tolerance**

   Components in scalable AI systems can fail owing to hardware faults or software bugs. Maintaining system availability requires ensuring fault tolerance and redundancy.

   Consideration: Using procedures such as automatic failover, in which a backup component takes over in the event of a breakdown, improves system reliability.

5. **Auto-Scaling**

   Auto-scaling, or the capacity to dynamically add or remove resources based on demand, is a crucial prerequisite for scalable AI systems.

   Consideration: Auto-scaling technologies in cloud-based services can automatically modify the number of instances or containers to handle shifting demands.

6. **Data Consistency**

   Maintaining data consistency across several copies of an application can be difficult in distributed AI systems, but it is critical for correct results.

   Consideration: Employing distributed databases or consensus techniques like Raft to assist in assuring data consistency

7. **Cost-Effectiveness**

   While scalability is critical, cost optimization is equally vital. To prevent excessive costs, scalable AI systems should make optimal use of resources.

   Consideration: Implementing resource monitoring and cost optimization measures can aid in the successful management of cloud infrastructure expenditures.

Scalable AI systems are the foundation of modern artificial intelligence–based applications. Design patterns are critical in attaining modularity, adaptability, and resource efficiency to meet the changing demands of data volume, model complexity, and user expectations. However, developing scalable AI systems is not without difficulties. Meeting data velocity requirements, ensuring low-latency responsiveness, and sustaining fault tolerance are all key factors.

OK, now let's summarize our learning from this chapter:

- Scalability is essential in AI systems, ensuring efficiency in handling increased workloads, data volumes, and user expectations.

- Scalable AI systems efficiently manage big data, respond to real-time user demands, support business expansion, and optimize costs.

- Netflix's recommendation system serves as an example, adapting to growing datasets during peak usage, providing personalized recommendations.

- Key considerations for scalability include load balancing, data partitioning, fault tolerance, auto-scaling, and data consistency.

- Practical examples, like load balancing in online shopping platforms, emphasize the importance of these considerations.

- Scalability dimensions include performance, vertical, data, model, operational, platform, and hybrid scalability.

- Real-world examples illustrate how each dimension applies, such as an ecommerce platform's recommendation system showcasing performance scalability.

- Challenges in managing data volume, handling model complexity, ensuring responsiveness, and optimizing costs are addressed.

- Practical considerations like data partitioning and containerization technologies (Docker, Kubernetes) are discussed to overcome challenges.

- Design patterns (Observer, Strategy, Factory) play a crucial role in achieving modularity, adaptability, and resource efficiency in scalable AI systems.

- Real-world applications, such as using the Observer Pattern in a recommendation system, highlight the practical utility of design patterns.

–   The chapter establishes a foundation for understanding scalable AI systems, covering theoretical concepts, real-world examples, and practical considerations.

–   Subsequent chapters will delve into scalability dimensions, design patterns, and emerging technologies, offering a comprehensive guide for building robust AI solutions.

# CHAPTER 2

# Fundamentals of Scalability in AI

Scalability in AI is analogous to making your favorite cookie recipe for a small family gathering and then seamlessly scaling up to create enough for a large party without sacrificing taste or quality. It means ensuring that your AI system can manage more data, more users, or more sophisticated jobs without breaking down.

Handling large datasets is a critical aspect of scalability in AI. Large datasets can be overwhelming, but with the right techniques, you can manage them effectively. Handling large datasets in AI is like managing a library with millions of books.

You need efficient techniques to organize, access, and analyze all that information without getting overwhelmed. Let's explore some easy-to-understand techniques, use cases, and examples.

## Why Handling Large Datasets Matters

Large datasets are the lifeblood of many AI applications, from recommendation systems to image recognition.

Here's why effectively handling them is crucial:

- **Better AI Models**: More data frequently leads to better AI models. AI systems learn from data, and the more high-quality data you have, the more accurate your models may be.

- **Improved Insights**: Large datasets can show patterns and insights that smaller datasets may overlook. This can be quite useful for making informed decisions.

© Abhishek Mishra 2024
A. Mishra, *Scalable AI and Design Patterns*, https://doi.org/10.1007/979-8-8688-0158-7_2

- **Real-World Applications**: Many real-world problems include massive volumes of data, such as healthcare records, financial transactions, or social media posts. The ability to handle big datasets is critical for the practical use of AI.

- **Competitive Advantage**: Organizations that can efficiently handle and use massive datasets acquire a competitive advantage in a variety of industries.

# Techniques for Handling Large Datasets

Let's delve into techniques for handling large datasets in artificial intelligence; we will go through code examples in the Python language:

1. **Explanation of Data Sampling**: You choose a representative sample rather than using the complete dataset. It's similar to judging the overall flavor of a large pot of soup by tasting a tiny bit of it.

   Consider the following scenario: You have a vast collection of customer reviews. Instead of analyzing them all at once, you select a smaller group at random. This subset should keep the dataset's diversity and qualities.

   Example code:

   ```
   import pandas as pd

   # Load a large dataset
   data = pd.read_csv('large_dataset.csv')

   # Randomly sample 10% of the data
   sampled_data = data.sample(frac=0.1)
   ```

2. **Explanation of Data Preprocessing and Cleaning**: Large datasets may contain noise, missing values, or discrepancies. Data preparation entails cleaning and modifying data so that it is ready for analysis.

   It's like having to tidy and clean a cluttered space before you can work in it.

In an image recognition task, you may have a dataset with photos of varying sizes. For consistency, all images are resized to a uniform dimension during preprocessing.

Example code:

```
from PIL import Image
import os
# Clean and preprocess a directory of images
def preprocess_images(input_dir, output_dir, target_
size=(224, 224)):
    for filename in os.listdir(input_dir):
        img = Image.open(os.path.join(input_dir, filename))
        img = img.resize(target_size)
        img.save(os.path.join(output_dir, filename))

# Usage
preprocess_images('input_images', 'output_images')
```

3.  **Data Streaming Explanation**: Rather than putting the entire dataset into memory, you handle it in smaller, more manageable portions or streams. It's like reading a book one chapter at a time rather than trying to read the entire book at once.

    Use case: If you're analyzing Twitter data in real time, you might analyze tweets as they arrive rather than waiting to collect all of them and then analyzing them.

    Example code:

```
# Process data from a file in chunks
chunk_size = 1000
with open('large_file.txt', 'r') as file:
    while True:
        data_chunk = file.read(chunk_size)
        if not data_chunk:
            break
        # Process the chunk
```

4. **Explanation of Parallel Processing**: Divide the dataset into smaller pieces and process them concurrently on several processors or devices. It's similar to having a group of people working on different aspects of a large project.

   Use case: When building a machine learning model, you can divide the data into subsets and train various parts on different machines, which speeds up the training process.

   Example code:

```
from multiprocessing import Pool

# Define a function to process data
def process_data(data_chunk):
    # Process the data_chunk here

# Split the dataset
data_chunks = split_large_dataset(large_data)

# Create a pool of worker processes
with Pool(processes=4) as pool:
    results = pool.map(process_data, data_chunks)
```

5. **Distributed Computing Explanation**: This is similar to having numerous libraries in different locations, and librarians can collaborate to find books rapidly. Data is distributed among numerous machines in AI, and they collaborate.

   Assume you're running a recommendation system for an ecommerce business. Distributing user and product data across numerous servers may assure speedy and efficient suggestions, even for millions of users.

**Dask Library Overview**

1. **Purpose**

   Definition: Dask is a Python library for parallel and distributed computing, designed to handle larger-than-memory datasets efficiently.

2. **Core Features**

   **Parallel Computing**: Breaks tasks into smaller operations for parallel execution, optimizing CPU and memory usage

   **Components**: Includes Dask Arrays, Dask DataFrames, Dask Bags, and Dask Delayed for handling different data structures

3. **Parallel Computing with Dask**

   **Task Graph**: Constructs a dynamic task graph for parallel execution, making it scalable for big data processing
   **Integration**: Seamlessly integrates with NumPy, Pandas, and scikit-learn for easy adoption

4. **Dask.distributed**

   **Cluster Computing**: Extends Dask for distributed computing across clusters, enhancing scalability

5. **Use Cases**

   **Big Data Processing**: Ideal for processing large datasets exceeding memory capacity

   **Parallelizing Code**: Easily parallelizes existing Python code for efficiency

   Example code:

```
from dask import dataframe as dd
# Load a large dataset with Dask
data = dd.read_csv('large_dataset.csv')
# Perform operations on the distributed dataframe
result = data.groupby('category').mean().compute()
```

6. **Data Indexing Explanation**: Just as you use an index to easily identify a specific topic in a book, data indexing entails constructing an index for your dataset. It enables speedier data retrieval.

   Use case: In a database of customer records, you can design an index based on customer IDs. When you need to get data for a certain consumer, the index speeds up the procedure significantly.

Example code:

```
import pandas as pd
# Load a large dataset
data = pd.read_csv('large_dataset.csv')

# Create an index based on a column (e.g., customer_id)
data_indexed = data.set_index('customer_id')
# Retrieve data by customer_id quickly
specific_data = data_indexed.loc['12345']
```

Handling huge datasets is a basic part of artificial intelligence. You may successfully handle and analyze large amounts of data by using techniques such as data sampling, preprocessing, streaming, parallel processing, distributed computing, and data indexing. Understanding these strategies and their applications is critical for developing strong AI systems capable of dealing with real-world situations.

These tactics can help you make sense of the data deluge and generate valuable insights, whether you're working on recommendation systems, picture recognition, or data analysis.

# Distributed Computing for Scalability

Distributed computing is similar to having a group of specialists collaborate to solve a large problem rather than depending on a single super-expert. In the context of AI scalability, this involves distributing jobs across numerous machines, allowing your AI system to perform more work without tiring.

### What Is Distributed Computing?

Distributed computing is a fancy way of expressing that rather than doing all of the computing on one computer, the work is distributed among numerous machines. Consider it a collaboration, with each machine performing a certain task.

### Why Distributed Computing Matters in Scalability

Assume you're making 100 cookies. Wouldn't it be much faster if you had ten ovens and could bake ten cookies at once? Distributed computing is similar to having ten ovens: it speeds up the process and increases the scalability of your AI system.

Explore the intricacies of model partitioning, delve into the capabilities of distributed computing frameworks like Ray and Dask, and grasp the collaborative essence of distributed artificial intelligence (DAI) for building robust and scalable AI solutions.

1. **Model Partitioning**

   Definition: Model partitioning is a strategy employed in scalable AI systems to distribute the computational workload of machine learning models across multiple devices or nodes. This is particularly crucial when dealing with large-scale models that might not fit into the memory of a single machine.

   Explanation: In model partitioning, a machine learning model is divided into smaller, manageable segments, and each segment is processed independently. This enables parallel processing, optimizing resource utilization. For example, in distributed deep learning, a neural network's layers can be assigned to different processing units, allowing for simultaneous computation.

   Example: Consider a deep neural network for image recognition. Model partitioning may involve assigning different convolutional layers to separate GPUs or nodes, allowing concurrent processing and accelerating overall model training.

2. **Distributed Computing Frameworks**

   a. Ray

   Definition: Ray is a general-purpose distributed computing framework for Python that facilitates parallel and distributed computing tasks. It provides a simple API for building distributed applications and supports a wide range of applications, including reinforcement learning, hyperparameter tuning, and distributed AI.

   Explanation: Ray's core features include task parallelism, distributed data processing, and a distributed object store. It allows users to parallelize existing Python code with minimal modifications. Ray's architecture supports dynamic task scheduling, making it suitable for applications with varying computational workloads.

Example: Ray can be used to parallelize tasks such as hyperparameter tuning for machine learning models. By distributing the parameter search across multiple nodes, Ray accelerates the optimization process.

b. Dask

Definition: Dask is a parallel computing library in Python designed for handling larger-than-memory datasets. It consists of Dask Arrays, Dask DataFrames, and other components that provide parallelized operations on data structures, making it suitable for scalable AI applications.

Explanation: Dask enables parallel and distributed computing by breaking down tasks into smaller operations that can be executed concurrently. It seamlessly integrates with popular Python libraries like NumPy and Pandas, making it a versatile choice for scaling existing workflows.

Example: Dask can be employed to process and analyze large datasets that don't fit into the memory of a single machine. By parallelizing operations on Dask DataFrames, it efficiently handles big data analytics.

3. **Distributed AI Approaches**

a. Distributed Artificial Intelligence (DAI)

Definition: Distributed artificial intelligence (DAI) refers to the paradigm of distributing AI tasks and computations across multiple nodes or devices. It involves collaborative processing, enabling the development of intelligent systems that leverage the collective capabilities of distributed components.

Explanation: DAI addresses challenges associated with the scale and complexity of AI tasks by distributing the workload. It enhances scalability, fault tolerance, and resource utilization. DAI frameworks often involve the use of communication protocols and coordination mechanisms for effective collaboration.

Example: In a distributed sensor network for autonomous vehicles, DAI can be applied to collectively process and analyze sensor data from multiple vehicles. Each vehicle contributes to the overall perception and decision-making process, resulting in a more robust and intelligent system.

# Techniques for Distributed Computing

Let us look at several approaches to better understand distributed computing:

1. **Simplicity**

   Parallelism is analogous to having several chefs working on different aspects of the same food at the same time. It refers to breaking down a large work into smaller sections and solving them all at once in distributed computing.

   Consider counting the number of times the word "cat" appears in a large book. Instead of reading the entire book, you may have nine pals count a tenth of it. You total their results when they're finished. This is an example of parallelism at work.

   Example code:

```
from multiprocessing import Pool
# Define a function to count words
def count_word(word, text):
    return text.count(word)

# Split the text into smaller chunks
text = "This is a big book with many words..."
chunks = [text[i:i+10] for i in range(0, len(text), 10)]

# Create a pool of workers
with Pool(10) as p:
    # Use parallelism to count the word in each chunk
    counts = p.starmap(count_word, [("cat", chunk) for chunk in
    chunks])
```

```
# Sum up the counts from each chunk
total_count = sum(counts)
print(total_count)
```

2. **Distributed Databases**

   Distributed databases are analogous to having multiple librarians administer various areas of a large library. Each librarian is in charge of their department, making it easier and faster to find books.

   For example, if you're developing a recommendation system, you might have user and product data kept in separate databases. Distributed databases allow you to keep these databases on separate servers, making data retrieval and processing faster.

3. **Queues for Messages**

   Message queues are similar to post offices in that you can transmit messages to be processed. Messages can be picked up and worked on separately by many workers.

   In a customer service AI system, for example, when customers submit inquiries, they are routed to a message queue. Multiple AI agents can then select questions from the queue and respond. This guarantees that user queries are handled efficiently.

   Example code:

```
from celery import Celery

# Initialize a Celery worker
app = Celery('myapp', broker='pyamqp://guest@localhost//')

# Define a task to process messages
@app.task
def process_message(message):
    # Process the message here
    return "Processed: " + message
```

```
# Send a message to the queue
message = "How can I reset my password?"
result = process_message.apply_async(args=[message])
print(result.get())
```

# Flow Diagram for Distributed Computing in Scalable AI

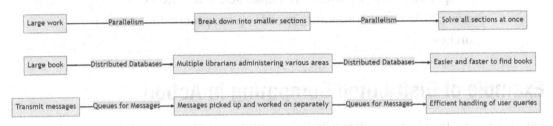

***Figure 2-1.*** *Flow diagram for distributed computing*

# Use Cases for Distributed Computing

Distributed computing can be applied to various AI use cases to achieve scalability:

1. **NLP (Natural Language Processing)**

   Language translation and sentiment analysis are two examples
   of computationally difficult NLP activities. Because distributed
   computing allows you to process multiple language requests at
   the same time, systems like Google Translate can be quick and
   scalable.

2. **Image and Video Editing**

   When dealing with huge photos or movies, tasks such as object
   detection or video analysis can be divided among numerous
   machines to accelerate the process. This is utilized in security
   surveillance systems as well as content recommendation services
   such as YouTube.

3. **Recommendation Engines**

   Distributed computing aids in the analysis of user behavior and
   product data in recommendation engines such as those used by
   Netflix and Amazon. It ensures that recommendations, even for
   millions of users and goods, are generated rapidly.

4. **Internet Search Engines**

   Every day, search engines like Google process billions of searches.
   By dispersing indexing and search tasks across a network of
   servers, distributed computing speeds up the processing of these
   searches.

# Example of Distributed Computing in Action

Let's take a practical example to see how distributed computing works in action. Imagine
you're building a distributed sentiment analysis system.

Real-time sentiment analysis of tweets (positive, negative, or neutral)

**Components**

**Data Collector**: Gathers tweets from multiple sources (such as the
Twitter API) and stores them in a message queue.

**Worker Nodes**: These are several machines, each with an AI
model for sentiment analysis. They separately select tweets from
the queue and analyze their mood.

**Result Aggregator**: Gathers sentiment analysis results from
worker nodes and produces overall sentiment statistics.

**Workflows**

A tweet is gathered and added to the message queue.

Worker nodes read tweets from the queue and assess their sentiment.

The sentiment analysis result is returned by each worker node.

These results are collected by the result aggregator, which creates overall
sentiment data.

This distributed system is scalable since it can manage a high volume of tweets and
deliver real-time sentiment analysis.

Distributed computing is an effective method for achieving scalability in AI. It's like having a team of specialists collaborate to complete a large task. You can make your AI system handle greater workloads more efficiently by splitting down tasks, leveraging parallelism, and distributing work over numerous processors. This is critical for AI applications that must evolve and adapt to changing needs, such as NLP jobs and recommendation systems.

# Parallel Processing Techniques and Scaling AI Models

Parallel processing is analogous to a group of friends collaborating to solve a large puzzle. Each friend works on their piece, and when they're finished, you join them all together to view the entire picture. Parallel processing in AI refers to breaking down a huge task into smaller sections and tackling them all at once. This enables AI models to manage larger workloads more efficiently.

### Why Use Parallel Processing in AI?

Assume you have a stack of 1000 arithmetic papers to grade. It would take you a long time if you did it one at a time. You could finish considerably faster if you had ten friends to assist you. Similarly, parallel processing can assist AI models because of the following:

> It **increases the speed** of tasks. Instead of waiting for one activity to be completed, you can work on several at once.

> **Scalability**: By dividing the task, AI models can handle larger datasets or more complicated problems.

> **Resource Efficiency**: Parallel processing enables AI to make efficient use of several processors or machines, which can save time and money.

# Techniques for Parallel Processing in AI

Here are some techniques used to implement parallel processing in AI:

1. **Parallelism in Data**

   Data parallelism is analogous to having multiple chefs prepare the same recipe for different dishes at the same time. In AI, this is breaking down the dataset into smaller bits and processing each one separately.

Data parallelism can be implemented using Python's multiprocessing package. Here's a simple example of parallel processing in Python using data parallelism:

Example code:

```
import multiprocessing
def process_data(chunk):
    # Process the data in this chunk
    pass

if __name__ == "__main__":
    data = get_large_dataset()
    num_processors = multiprocessing.cpu_count()
    pool = multiprocessing.Pool(processes=num_processors)
    results = pool.map(process_data, data)
    pool.close()
    pool.join()
```

In this code, the multiprocessing library is used to process data chunks in parallel, utilizing all available CPU cores.

2. **Parallelism in Models**

Model parallelism is analogous to having multiple specialists working on separate aspects of a complex task. It is used in AI for models that cannot fit inside a single machine's memory.

Technique: Frameworks such as TensorFlow and PyTorch can be used to distribute a large model across numerous GPUs or workstations. Here's an example of TensorFlow in action:

Example code:

```
import tensorflow as tf

# Build and compile the model
model = create_large_model()
model.compile(optimizer='adam', loss='sparse_categorical_
crossentropy', metrics=['accuracy'])
```

```
# Split the model across multiple GPUs
strategy = tf.distribute.MirroredStrategy()
with strategy.scope():
    parallel_model = create_parallel_model(model)
```

```
# Train the model in parallel
parallel_model.fit(train_data, epochs=10)
```

In this code, the model is split across multiple GPUs using TensorFlow's MirroredStrategy, allowing you to train a large model in parallel.

3. **Task Sequencing**

   Task parallelism is equivalent to having multiple teams work on various components of a project. In AI, it entails breaking down a large work into smaller subtasks that may be processed concurrently.

   Technique: For distributed task processing, task parallelism can be achieved utilizing libraries such as Celery or Apache Kafka. Here's an example of how to use Celery in Python:

   Example code:

```
from celery import Celery
```

```
app = Celery('myapp', broker='pyamqp://guest@localhost//')
```

```
@app.task
def process_task(task_data):
    # Process the task
    pass
```

```
# Create and distribute tasks
for task_data in large_task_list:
    process_task.delay(task_data)
```

In this code, tasks are processed concurrently by worker processes managed by Celery.

# Challenges in Parallel Processing

While parallel processing has numerous advantages, it also has certain drawbacks:

1. **Harmonization**

   When many processes or threads work on separate sections of an issue, their actions must be coordinated. Synchronization problems might result in errors or inefficiency.

   For example, if two parallel processes write to the same file at the same time, their data may be overwritten.

2. **Load Distribution**

   For efficient parallel processing, jobs must be distributed evenly among processors. Load imbalances might cause some processors to finish early while others continue to work.

   In a data parallelism scenario, for example, if one CPU is given a substantially larger block of data to process, it may take longer to complete its work.

3. **Communication Overhead**

   There may be communication overhead when various processes must share information. This has the potential to slow down parallel processing.

In a distributed system, for example, if nodes frequently exchange large amounts of data, this might cause network congestion and impede processing.

Parallel processing is a key method that enables AI models to efficiently handle greater workloads. It breaks down tasks into smaller chunks and processes them all at once, resulting in speedier and more scalable AI systems. AI developers can benefit from parallel processing by using techniques such as data parallelism, model parallelism, and task parallelism.

However, addressing synchronization, load balancing, and communication overhead issues is critical to ensuring the seamless operation of parallel AI systems. Parallel processing, when implemented intelligently, can assist AI models in solving complicated problems more rapidly and effectively.

# Scaling AI Models: Making Big AI Work for Everyone

Scaling AI models entails making them larger, more powerful, and capable of handling more complex tasks. It's the same as going from a simple laptop to a supercomputer. Models in AI are similar to recipes that computers use to solve issues. Scaling these models entails making those recipes more sophisticated to address larger and more difficult issues.

## Why Scaling AI Models Matters

Scaling AI models is essential for several reasons:

**Complex Tasks**: Some tasks, like interpreting human language or image processing, necessitate vast computational capacity. AI can now solve these hard tasks because of scaling.

**Better Accuracy**: Because larger models can learn from more data, they can make more accurate predictions or classifications.

Scaling can result in more **efficient AI systems** since they can process jobs faster, saving time and resources.

Large-scale AI models can be fine-tuned for specific tasks, making **AI more adaptable**.

## Techniques for Scaling AI Models

Here are some techniques used to scale AI models:

1. **Model Architectures**

   Choose bigger and more complex model architectures. One famous example is OpenAI's GPT-3, which has 175 billion parameters, making it one of the largest AI models.

2. **Parallel Processing**

   Split tasks into smaller pieces and process them simultaneously. It's like having a team of chefs working together in the kitchen.

3. **Distributed Computing**

   Spread the workload across multiple machines or servers. It's like having a network of chefs working together in different kitchens.

4. **Quantization**

   Quantization means representing numbers with fewer bits. It reduces the memory and computation needed to run large models.

Scaling AI models is essential for realizing their full potential. We may address increasingly difficult challenges across multiple domains by making models larger, more sophisticated, and more efficient.

Scaling AI models, whether for natural language processing, computer vision, or recommendation systems, enables us to construct smarter, more competent AI systems. Remember that while scaling has numerous advantages, it also has drawbacks in terms of processing resources, data handling, and optimization.

Balancing these characteristics is critical for realizing the full potential of scaled AI models.

Let's summarize our learning from this chapter. Scalability in AI is crucial for managing increased data, users, and tasks without sacrificing quality. Efficient techniques for organizing, accessing, and analyzing large datasets are essential. The significance of large datasets lies in improving AI model quality, gaining insights, and addressing real-world challenges, providing a competitive advantage.

Handling techniques encompass data sampling, preprocessing, data streaming, parallel processing, distributed computing, and data indexing. The Dask library, a Python tool for parallel and distributed computing, seamlessly integrates with popular libraries like NumPy and Pandas.

Distributed computing finds application in NLP, image/video editing, recommendation engines, and Internet search engines. An example involves real-time sentiment analysis of tweets using components like data collector, worker nodes, and result aggregator.

Parallel processing techniques—data, model, and task parallelism—are utilized in AI to enhance speed, scalability, and resource efficiency. However, challenges like synchronization and load distribution must be addressed.

Scaling AI models involves making them larger, more powerful, and efficient. Techniques include choosing larger architectures, implementing parallel processing, utilizing distributed computing, and employing quantization. Balancing resources, data handling, and optimization is critical for maximizing the potential of scaled AI models.

# CHAPTER 3

# Data Engineering for Scalable AI

In today's digital world, data is everywhere. Data is being generated at an unprecedented rate, from your social media interactions to Internet purchases and healthcare records to weather forecasts. This huge volume of data has become the lifeblood of modern enterprises and technologies, particularly artificial intelligence (AI). But, to harness the power of this data and construct scalable AI systems, we need a solid foundation in data engineering.

Data engineering is the process of gathering, converting, and transmitting data from diverse sources into a format that can be used for analysis, reporting, and, in this case, training and deploying AI models. It serves as the foundation for data-driven decision-making.

Consider a social media network such as Facebook. Every day, it captures massive quantities of data, including your posts, likes, and friend requests. Data engineers create systems to efficiently store and handle this data so that Facebook's AI algorithms can display relevant content and adverts.

## Why Is Data Engineering Important for AI?

Data is required for AI systems, such as machine learning models, to learn and predict. The quantity and quality of data have a substantial impact on AI performance. AI systems require clean, well-organized, and up-to-date data, which data engineering ensures. AI would be like a car without fuel if it didn't have good data engineering. Data engineering revolves around the data life cycle, which consists of several stages:

© Abhishek Mishra 2024
A. Mishra, *Scalable AI and Design Patterns*, https://doi.org/10.1007/979-8-8688-0158-7_3

### Data Collection

The process of creating or acquiring data is referred to as data generation. This can include data generated by IoT (Internet of Things) devices, sensor readings, or user interactions on websites.

For example, every time you make an online purchase, your transaction history creates data. This information includes what you purchased, when you purchased it, and where it was transported.

### Ingestion of Data

Data ingestion entails gathering information from numerous sources and transferring it to a single location for processing. This is analogous to gathering ingredients before preparing a meal.

For example, a retailer collects information from its website, mobile app, and in-store sales terminals. Data engineers create pipelines to collect and store this data in a centralized database.

### Data Storage

When data is absorbed, it needs a secure location to reside. Data storage entails selecting the appropriate storage system, whether it's a standard relational database or a modern distributed storage system like Hadoop HDFS.

For example, Netflix uses a distributed storage system to keep data about its members' viewing patterns. This enables them to analyze the data and offer personalized content recommendations.

### Data Processing

Raw data frequently need to be translated into a more usable format. This could include cleaning, aggregating, or enhancing the data.

For example, a weather forecasting service collects raw weather data from numerous sensors. Data engineers use this information to generate projections and visualizations that people can understand.

### Data Analysis

Data analysis is where the magic happens. Data scientists and AI models use processed data to gain insights and make predictions.

For example, data scientists in a healthcare company examine patient records to identify trends and construct predictive models for disease outbreaks.

### Data Visualization

Data is useless if it cannot be comprehended. Data visualization converts complex data into charts, graphs, and dashboards that anybody can understand.

For example, a stock trading platform employs data visualization to show traders real-time stock prices and trends.

# Data Ingestion and Preprocessing at Scale

The process of collecting and importing data from numerous sources into a storage or processing system is known as data ingestion. Data ingestion pipelines must be efficient and resilient to enable scaled AI systems. Here are some examples of practices and strategies:

1. **Streaming Data Ingestion Practice**: To ingest data in real time, use streaming data systems such as Apache Kafka or Amazon Kinesis.

   Assume you're tracking social media mentions of your brand. Streaming data solutions provide real-time responses by capturing and analyzing mentions as they occur.

   Example code: Apace Kafka in Python

   ```
   from kafka import KafkaConsumer
   consumer = KafkaConsumer('social_mentions', bootstrap_
   servers='kafka-server:9092')
   for message in consumer:
       print(message.value)
   ```

2. **Practice Batch Data Ingestion**: Use batch data ingestion for periodic updates and historical data.

   Explanation: Batch data ingestion is useful when analyzing data over a longer period, such as sales trends over the past year.

   Example Python code (with pandas):

   ```
   import pandas as pd
   data = pd.read_csv('sales_data.csv')
   ```

3. **Data Validation and Schema Enforcement**: Validate incoming data to verify it meets the required schema and quality requirements.

   Explanation: It is critical to prevent corrupt or mismatched data from entering your system to ensure data integrity.

   Advanced technique: Define and enforce data structures using Apache Avro or Apache Thrift.

Data preprocessing entails cleaning, manipulating, and enriching data to make it appropriate for AI modeling. Here are several best practices, strategies, and advanced methodologies for effective data preprocessing:

1. **Data Cleaning Practice**: Identify and handle missing or inconsistent data.

   Explanation: Incomplete or erroneous data might lead to biased AI models or wrong predictions.

   Advanced technique: To fill in missing values, use statistical imputation methods such as mean, median, or regression.

   Example code (using Python and pandas):

```
# Fill missing values with the mean
data['age'].fillna(data['age'].mean(), inplace=True)
```

2. **Practice Feature Scaling and Normalization**: Scale numerical features to ensure that they have similar scales, preventing some features from dominating the model.

   Explanation: In an AI model, without scaling, a parameter like "income" (in thousands) can overwhelm a feature like "age" (in years).

   Advanced technique: For feature scaling, use min-max scaling or standardization (Z-score normalization).

   Example code (using Python and scikit-learn):

```
from sklearn.preprocessing import MinMaxScaler

scaler = MinMaxScaler()
data[['income', 'age']] = scaler.fit_transform(data[['income',
'age']])
```

3. **One-Hot Encoding Practice**: Using one-hot encoding, convert categorical variables to numerical representation.

   Explanation: Because machine learning models require numerical input, category variables such as "color" must be converted into binary values (0 or 1).

   Advanced technique: For high-cardinality categorical variables, use category embeddings.

   Example code (using Python and pandas):

```
data = pd.get_dummies(data, columns=['color'])
```

4. **Text Data Preprocessing Practice**: Process and clean text data for natural language processing (NLP) activities.

   Text data frequently necessitates tokenization, lowercasing, and the removal of stopwords and special characters.

   Advanced technique: For NLP jobs, use techniques like lemmatization or word embeddings (Word2Vec or GloVe).

   Example code (using Python and NLTK for text tokenization):

```
from nltk.tokenize import word_tokenize
text = "This is an example sentence."
tokens = word_tokenize(text)
```

5. **Parallel Processing Practice**: Use parallel processing or distributed computing frameworks like Apache Spark to preprocess data faster, especially for huge datasets.

   Explanation: Parallel processing breaks data into smaller bits and processes them concurrently, considerably lowering preprocessing time.

Advanced technique: Use parallelization libraries such as Dask or multiprocessing in Python to implement parallelization.

Example code (using Dask in Python for parallel processing):

```
import dask.dataframe as dd

ddf = dd.from_pandas(data, npartitions=4)  # Create a Dask
DataFrame
result = ddf.groupby('category').mean().compute()  # Parallelized
computation
```

# Case Studies

To put these practices and advanced procedures into context, consider the following real-world examples:

1. **Recommendation Systems for Ecommerce**

   Data ingestion: Streaming website user interactions and batch importing past purchase data.

   Cleaning and processing user behavior data, one-hot encoding product categories, and applying collaborative filtering algorithms for suggestions are all examples of data preprocessing.

2. **Healthcare Predictive Analytics Data Ingestion**

   Collecting real-time patient records from hospitals and batching research papers and medical literature.

   Data preprocessing includes cleaning and validating patient data, using natural language processing to extract relevant information from research articles, and developing predictive models for disease diagnosis. Data ingestion and preprocessing are the unsung heroes of scalable AI systems.

# Feature Engineering for Scalable AI

Feature engineering is the art and science of identifying, modifying, and producing appropriate features (data properties) for machine learning models. When it comes to scalable AI systems, successful feature engineering is akin to building a strong bridge that can withstand the weight of complex algorithms and large datasets.

Simply said, feature engineering is the process of making your data function better for your AI models. It entails

- **Choosing the Right Features**: Determining which features of your data are relevant to the problem at hand

- **Transforming Features**: Converting data into a format that machine learning algorithms can understand

- **Adding New Features**: Adding new features to the current data to improve model performance

# What Is the Importance of Feature Engineering in Scalable AI?

Consider creating a recommendation system for an ecommerce website. To produce reliable product suggestions for millions of consumers, different aspects such as user behavior, product qualities, and time of day must be considered. Feature engineering assists you in creating meaningful features from these parameters that your recommendation model can simply digest, resulting in an accurate and scalable system.

# Practices and Strategies for Feature Engineering

1. **Understanding the Problem**

   Before getting into feature engineering, make sure you understand the problem you're attempting to solve. What are the key factors influencing the outcome? This comprehension will drive your feature selection and development.

For example, understanding that the choice of words and the sender's address are important aspects of a spam email classifier will help you pick which features to utilize.

2.  **EDA (Exploratory Data Analysis)**

    EDA is similar to exploring a treasure map before going treasure hunting. Visualizing and comprehending your data aids in the identification of patterns and outliers that can drive feature engineering decisions.

3.  **Selection and Scaling of Features**

    Not all characteristics are equally important. Some may introduce noise into your model or result in overfitting. To choose the most relevant features, use approaches such as correlation analysis or feature importance ratings.

    Scaling guarantees that your machine learning system treats features with different units or magnitudes equally. Min-max scaling and standardization (Z-score normalization) are two common strategies.

4.  **Categorical Data Handling**

    Numerical data is frequently required for machine learning models. Encoding techniques such as one-hot encoding or label encoding are used to convert categorical features (such as "red," "green," and "blue") into numerical form.

5.  **Time Series Data Feature Engineering**

    Time series data demands specific consideration. To capture temporal patterns, elements like rolling averages, time delays, and seasonality indicators can be created.

6.  **Feature Development**

    Creating additional features can sometimes greatly increase model performance. This requires domain knowledge as well as inventiveness.

For example, in a fraud detection system, you could include a function that estimates the average transaction value for each user, assisting in the identification of anomalous spending patterns.

# Advanced Feature Engineering Techniques

1. **Neural Networks for Feature Extraction**

   Deep learning models can discover meaningful features directly from raw data, avoiding the need for traditional feature engineering. For this purpose, Convolutional Neural Networks (CNNs) for images and Recurrent Neural Networks (RNNs) for sequences are effective.

   Example code (Python—using TensorFlow/Keras):

   ```python
   from tensorflow.keras.layers import Conv2D
   from tensorflow.keras.layers import LSTM

   # Define a CNN layer for image feature extraction
   cnn_model = Sequential()
   cnn_model.add(Conv2D(32, (3, 3), activation='relu', input_
   shape=(64, 64, 3)))

   # Define an LSTM layer for sequence feature extraction
   lstm_model = Sequential()
   lstm_model.add(LSTM(100, input_shape=(X.shape[1], X.shape[2])))
   ```

2. **Automated Feature Engineering**

   AutoML tools like Featuretools and TPOT can automatically generate and select features, saving time and effort.

   Example code (Python—using Featuretools):

   ```python
   import featuretools as ft

   # Create an entity set
   es = ft.EntitySet(id="data")
   ```

```
# Add entities and relationships
es = es.entity_from_dataframe(entity_id="data", dataframe=data,
index="index")
es = es.normalize_entity(base_entity_id="data", new_entity_
id="user", index="user_id")

# Generate features
feature_matrix, feature_defs = ft.dfs(entityset=es, target_
entity="data", agg_primitives=["mean", "max"], trans_
primitives=["month", "weekday"])
```

3. **Embedding for Categorical Data**

   Word embeddings, like Word2Vec, can be adapted for categorical data to create meaningful representations.

   Example code (Python—using Gensim):

   ```
   from gensim.models import Word2Vec

   model = Word2Vec(sentences=data['category'], vector_size=10,
   window=5, min_count=1)
   category_embedding = model.wv['electronics']
   ```

Feature engineering is a critical stage in the development of scalable AI systems. It combines art, science, and subject knowledge. Understanding your problem, exploring your data, and employing the appropriate methodologies can enable your AI models to make accurate predictions and recommendations even in the face of massive amounts of data. Remember that feature engineering is an iterative process and that constant refining is essential in the field of scalable AI.

# Data Storage and Management Strategies

A solid foundation for data storage and management is critical in the field of artificial intelligence (AI). Your data's quality, accessibility, and scalability can make or ruin your AI efforts.

**What is the definition of data storage and management?**

Data storage relates to where and how you keep your data. Databases, file systems, cloud storage, or a combination of these are all possibilities. Data management entails the processes and tools used to organize, store, retrieve, and secure your data.

# Storage Scalability in Data

Scalability means that your data storage can increase to meet your changing needs. Consider the following while designing scalable AI systems:

1. **Scaling Horizontally**

   As data expands, horizontal scaling entails adding more machines or nodes to your storage system. It's analogous to expanding a parking lot by adding more parking spaces rather than increasing the size of each parking place.

   As an example, consider using distributed databases such as Cassandra to store user data. You can add more servers to handle the increased load as more users sign up.

2. **Scaling Vertically**

   Vertical scaling is the process of updating existing equipment to handle heavier workloads. It's similar to increasing the RAM on a computer to help it run faster.

Increasing the memory on your database server, for example, to store and analyze more data efficiently.

# Data Storage Methodologies

Some key data storage solutions for scalable AI systems are as follows:

1. **Select the Appropriate Database Type**

   It is critical to select the appropriate database. Consider the following:

   SQL databases are ideal for organized data with well-defined relationships. Consider PostgreSQL.

   NoSQL databases are best suited to unstructured or semi-structured data. Consider MongoDB.

2. **Data Segmentation**

Partitioning is the process of splitting your data into smaller sections. Each split can be kept on a separate server. This helps to spread the data load and improve query performance.

For instance, if you have a client database, you may partition it by geographical location to lessen the strain on your servers.

3. **Compression of Data**

Data compression lowers storage costs and speeds up data retrieval.

Example: Storing log files in a compressed format to save space while still allowing quick access when needed.

4. **Indexing of Data**

Indexing facilitates faster data retrieval. It's similar to a book's index, which takes you to the specific page where a topic is presented.

In a product catalog, for example, constructing an index on product IDs enables quick lookups when users search for specific products.

# Advanced Methods

Now, let's look at some advanced data storage and management techniques:

1. **Storage in Columns**

Columnar databases, as opposed to rows, store data in columns. This speeds up aggregations and analytics.

Example (using Python and Pandas):

```
import pandas as pd
# Load data into a DataFrame
data = pd.read_csv('sales_data.csv')

# Perform a quick aggregation
total_sales_by_product = data.group by('product_name')
['sales_amount'].sum()
```

2. **Distributed Databases**

   Distributed databases spread data across multiple servers. This
   enhances both storage capacity and query performance.

   Example (using Amazon Redshift):

   ```
   -- Create a distributed table
   CREATE TABLE sales (
       sale_id INT,
       product_name VARCHAR(255),
       sale_amount DECIMAL
   ) DISTSTYLE KEY DISTKEY (sale_id);
   ```

3. **Data Lakes**

   Data lakes store data in its raw form, making it ideal for big data
   and AI. You can use tools like Apache Hadoop to process and
   analyze data from data lakes.

   Example (using Hadoop and Hive):

   ```
   -- Create an external table in Hive for querying data in a
   data lake
   CREATE EXTERNAL TABLE sales (
       sale_id INT,
       product_name STRING,
       sale_amount DOUBLE
   )
   ROW FORMAT DELIMITED FIELDS TERMINATED BY ','
   LOCATION '/data-lake/sales';
   ```

Scalable AI systems rely on effective data storage and management solutions.
Organizations can unlock the full potential of AI for a variety of applications, from
personalized recommendations to life-saving healthcare diagnostics and the future of
autonomous transportation, by grasping the fundamentals, implementing scalability
principles, and employing sophisticated approaches.

Remember that, while the techniques are evolving, the fundamental concepts of
data storage and management are still available to those prepared to investigate and
apply them.

Let's summarize our learning. This chapter provided an overview of data engineering for scalable AI. It emphasized the critical role of data in the digital world and its significance for artificial intelligence (AI). The chapter covered the data life cycle, including collection, ingestion, storage, processing, analysis, and visualization. It delved into data ingestion and preprocessing practices, with examples such as streaming and batch data ingestion. The case studies highlighted real-world applications in ecommerce recommendations and healthcare predictive analytics.

The importance of feature engineering for scalable AI was discussed, outlining practices, strategies, and advanced techniques. Feature engineering involves selecting, transforming, and adding features to improve machine learning model performance. The chapter also explored data storage and management strategies, emphasizing scalability principles, appropriate database selection, and advanced methods like storage in columns and data lakes. Overall, the chapter underscored the foundational role of effective data engineering in unlocking the full potential of AI across diverse applications.

You can explore the official documentation and architecture guides provided by each cloud service provider:

- **Google Cloud Platform (GCP)**

  GCP Architecture Center: `https://cloud.google.com/architecture`

- **Amazon Web Services (AWS)**

  AWS Architecture Center: `https://aws.amazon.com/architecture/`

- **Microsoft Azure**

  Azure Architecture Center: `https://docs.microsoft.com/en-us/azure/architecture/`

In these documentation centers, you'll find a wealth of information on scalable architectures, distributed computing, and best practices for designing and implementing various solutions on each cloud platform. Look for topics related to data engineering, AI, feature engineering, and scalable storage.

# CHAPTER 4

# Scalable AI Algorithms and Models

Artificial intelligence (AI) is becoming increasingly prevalent. AI is changing the way we live and work, from chatbots that assist with customer service to recommendation algorithms that suggest which films to watch. However, the strength of AI is derived from algorithms and models, not from magic. We'll look at what scalable AI algorithms and models are, why they're important, and how they function.

## What Are Scalable AI Algorithms and Models?

Let's start with the fundamentals. When we discuss AI algorithms and models, we are effectively discussing the brains of AI systems. These are the things that allow robots to execute activities that normally need human intellect, such as picture recognition, natural language interpretation, and prediction.

The term "scalable" now refers to the ability of these algorithms and models to handle a wide range of jobs, from simple to complicated, and to do so effectively. Consider a chef who can not only produce a single dish but also adapt and prepare a whole menu for a large restaurant. That chef, like scalable AI algorithms and models, is scalable. We discussed in previous chapters how scalable AI matters; let's understand how scalable AI algorithms and models work.

We'll break it down into three basic steps to explain:

1. **Model Training**

   A model is at the heart of many AI systems. Consider a model to be a mathematical structure capable of learning from data. During the training phase, this model is exposed to a large number of instances to understand patterns and relationships.

© Abhishek Mishra 2024
A. Mishra, *Scalable AI and Design Patterns*, https://doi.org/10.1007/979-8-8688-0158-7_4

Consider teaching a computer to recognize cats in photographs. You would show it thousands of cat photographs, allowing it to learn the characteristics that distinguish a cat.

2. **Making Predictions**

   Once trained, the model can make predictions or choices based on new data. This is where the AI begins to display its intellect. For instance, after training, our cat-recognition model can confidently say whether or not a new image contains a cat.

3. **Expanding**

   This is when the scalability comes into play. A scalable AI algorithm or model can be quickly altered or expanded to handle more difficult tasks or a bigger volume of data.

   For example, if you wanted to expand our cat-recognition model to recognize not only cats but also dogs, birds, and other animals, a scalable model could easily adapt to this new task.

# Unlocking Efficiency Through Distributed Computing and Model Optimization

Distributed algorithms facilitate seamless coordination among networked nodes, while model compression and distillation techniques ensure the deployment of lean yet powerful machine learning models. Additionally, ensemble learning techniques harness the collective intelligence of diverse models, collectively driving advancements in scalable AI systems.

### Distributed Algorithms

Distributed algorithms refer to computational algorithms designed for multiple machines or nodes in a network. They are crucial for coordinating tasks in distributed systems and ensuring synchronization and fault tolerance.

Explanation:

In a distributed system, nodes collaborate to achieve common goals. Distributed algorithms manage consensus, coordination, and fault tolerance across these nodes.

Examples:

**Paxos Algorithm**: Ensures consensus in unreliable processors

**MapReduce**: Enables parallel processing of large datasets in a distributed cluster

Use cases:

**Distributed Databases**: Coordinating transactions across multiple nodes

**Distributed File Systems**: Ensuring data consistency and availability

**Model Compression**

Model compression involves reducing the size of a machine learning model, making it lightweight and efficient without compromising performance. This is essential for deploying models on resource-constrained devices or for faster inference.

Explanation:

Large models may be impractical for deployment on edge devices or mobile apps. Model compression techniques aim to reduce the model size without significantly sacrificing accuracy.

Examples:

**Pruning**: Removing unnecessary weights or neurons

**Quantization**: Reducing precision of weights (e.g., from 32-bit floating point to 8-bit integer)

**Knowledge Distillation**: Training a smaller model to mimic a larger model

Use cases:

**Edge Devices**: Deploying models on IoT devices with limited storage

**Mobile Applications**: Reducing model size for efficient app deployment

### Model Distillation

Model distillation (or knowledge distillation) is a form of model compression where a smaller model is trained to replicate the behavior of a larger, more complex model.

Explanation:

It involves transferring knowledge from a complex teacher model to a simpler student model. This is achieved by training the student model to mimic the output patterns of the teacher model.

Examples:

> Training a compact neural network to mimic a larger pretrained model

> Distilling knowledge from an ensemble of models into a single model

Use cases:

> **Reducing Inference Latency**: Deploying a smaller model for faster predictions

> **Enabling On-Device Inference**: Suitable for edge computing

### Ensemble Learning

Ensemble learning combines predictions from multiple machine learning models to improve overall performance and generalization.

Explanation:

Ensemble methods reduce overfitting, increase accuracy, and enhance model stability by leveraging predictions from diverse models trained on different subsets or with different algorithms.

Examples:

> **Random Forest**: An ensemble of decision trees

> **Gradient Boosting**: Sequentially training models to correct errors

> **Voting Classifiers**: Combining predictions through a voting mechanism

Use cases:

**Classification Tasks**: Improving accuracy in tasks such as image classification

**Regression Problems**: Enhancing prediction accuracy in real-value prediction

# Types of Scalable AI Algorithms and Models

There are various types of scalable AI algorithms and models, each designed for specific tasks. Let's explore some common ones:

1. **Neural Networks**

   Neural networks are inspired by the human brain and are effective for tasks such as image and speech recognition. They are made up of layers of interconnected nodes (neurons) that process information.

   When you ask a voice assistant like Siri a question, it uses a neural network to transform your speech into text and analyze your query.

2. **Decision Trees**

   Decision trees are flowcharts that assist AI in making judgments based on given data. They are excellent for tasks that require you to make a sequence of decisions.

   For example, a decision tree can assist a medical diagnosis AI system in determining if a patient's symptoms indicate a typical cold or a more serious illness.

3. **Random Forests**

   Random forests are a collection of decision trees. They are ideal for activities that need a high level of accuracy and are frequently utilized in applications such as fraud detection.

Banks, for example, utilize random forests to identify possibly fraudulent transactions by analyzing several data such as transaction amount, location, and time.

4. **Natural Language Processing (NLP) Models**

   NLP models are intended to comprehend and generate human language. They're employed in chatbots, language translation, and sentiment analysis.

   When you use a language translation program to convert English text to French, it is most likely employing an NLP model.

5. **Reinforcement Learning Models**

   Reinforcement learning models learn by trial and error. They are employed in assignments where an AI agent must make judgments to maximize a reward. For example, DeepMind's AlphaGo, which beat the world champion in the game of Go, uses reinforcement learning to improve its gameplay.

# The Future of Scalable AI

Scalable AI algorithms and models are rapidly evolving. Here are some intriguing developments to look out for shortly:

1. **Democratization of AI**

   "AI democratization" refers to the increased availability and use of artificial intelligence techniques and technology to a broader audience. This trend intends to make AI more accessible to individuals and organizations outside of typical tech domains, hence fostering innovation across multiple industries. Cloud services provided by major platforms such as AWS, Azure, and GCP greatly contribute to this democratization by allowing consumers to utilize advanced AI capabilities without extensive knowledge. As AI becomes increasingly user-friendly and versatile, its integration into various applications and industries accelerates, paving the way for a future in which intelligent solutions are accessible to everybody.

2. **Explainable AI**

   Researchers are attempting to make artificial intelligence systems more transparent and explainable. This will assist users in comprehending why AI makes specific decisions.

   For example, a medical AI system could explain why it suggests a specific treatment.

3. **Artificial Intelligence in Creativity**

   AI is being utilized to develop fresh and original material in creative industries such as art, music, and writing.

   For instance, AI algorithms can compose music or create artwork based on a specific style or theme.

4. **Artificial Intelligence in Education**

   AI-powered education technologies are becoming increasingly common, providing students with personalized learning experiences.

   For instance, AI can analyze a student's performance and tailor the curriculum to their specific needs.

# Distributed Training Techniques

Distributed training is like teamwork for AI models. We will cover more on model parallelism in the chapters ahead. Instead of one computer doing all the work, multiple computers collaborate to train a model faster and more effectively. Here's how it works:

1. **Parallelism in Data**

   Assume you're making cookies and have a large amount of dough to combine. Data parallelism is analogous to having several bakers, each with their mixing bowl and ingredients. They all work at the same time, making the procedure significantly speedier.

   For example, if you're training an image recognition model on a large dataset, data parallelism would entail breaking the dataset into chunks and having each machine work its chunk at the same time.

```python
# TensorFlow code for data parallelism
import tensorflow as tf

# Create a model
model = tf.keras.Sequential([...])

# Define a dataset
dataset = tf.data.Dataset.from_tensor_slices([...])

# Split the dataset into shards for each device
num_devices = 4
datasets = dataset.shard(num_devices, 0)

# Create a strategy for distributed training
strategy = tf.distribute.MirroredStrategy()

# Create a model inside the strategy scope
with strategy.scope():
    model = create_model()

# Train the model
model.compile(optimizer='adam', loss='sparse_categorical_
crossentropy', metrics=['accuracy'])
model.fit(datasets, epochs=5)
```

2. **Parallelism in Models**

Model parallelism is similar to putting together a puzzle. Each computer works on a different piece of the puzzle (a different portion of the model), and when they're all finished, you fit the puzzle pieces together to view the entire picture (the trained model).

For example, in the training of a big language model such as GPT-3, separate machines may handle distinct elements of the model architecture.

3. **Server of Parameters**

Consider parameter servers to be librarians. They keep the model's parameters (knowledge) in one place, where multiple workers (computers) can request and update them as needed.

For example, in deep reinforcement learning, where AI agents learn through trial and error, parameter servers aid in the distribution of successful tactics among all agents.

```
# Parameter server pseudocode
while True:
    gradients = worker.compute_gradients(local_model)
    parameter_server.apply_gradients(gradients)
```

4. **Horovod**

Horovod is similar to an orchestra conductor. It organizes the activities of several devices (musicians) to efficiently train the AI model.

Horovod, for example, is a popular framework for distributed training that is frequently used with deep learning libraries such as TensorFlow and PyTorch.

```
# Horovod example for TensorFlow
import tensorflow as tf
import horovod.tensorflow as hvd

# Initialize Horovod
hvd.init()

# Build a model
model = tf.keras.Sequential([...])

# Optimizer
opt = tf.keras.optimizers.SGD(0.01 * hvd.size())

# Wrap the optimizer with Horovod
opt = hvd.DistributedOptimizer(opt)
```

```
# Compile the model
model.compile(optimizer=opt, loss='sparse_categorical_
crossentropy', metrics=['accuracy'])

# Train the model
model.fit(train_dataset, steps_per_epoch=steps_per_epoch, epochs=5)
```

# Approaches to Online Learning

Instead of relearning everything from scratch, online learning allows you to constantly update your knowledge as you encounter new material. It is extremely beneficial for AI systems that must adapt to changing data over time. Here are a few ideas:

1.  **SGD (Stochastic Gradient Descent)**

    SGD is like gradually fine-tuning a recipe as you bake more cookies. Instead of utilizing the same recipe for each batch, you tweak it somewhat based on the results of the prior batch.

    SGD, for example, is used in online advertising to update recommendation models as people engage with the site.

    ```
    # SGD pseudocode
    while True:
        batch = get_next_batch()
        gradients = compute_gradients(model, batch)
        model.update_parameters(gradients)
    ```

2.  **Mini-Batch Learning**

    Mini-batch learning is equivalent to studying a few pages of a book at a time rather than the entire book. You update the model based on a tiny fraction of the input, making learning faster and more adaptive.

    Mini-batch learning is often used in natural language processing to train chatbots that improve with each conversation.

```
# Mini-batch learning pseudocode
while True:
    mini_batch = get_next_mini_batch()
    gradients = compute_gradients(model, mini_batch)
    model.update_parameters(gradients)
```

3. **Reinforcement Learning**

   Reinforcement learning is analogous to teaching a dog new tricks. You give the dog incentives or penalties according to its actions, and it learns to behave better over time.

   In robotics, for example, reinforcement learning is used to educate robots to do tasks like choosing and placing objects.

```
# Reinforcement learning example using OpenAI Gym
import gym

# Create an environment
env = gym.make('CartPole-v1')

# Define and train an agent
```

4. **Online Clustering**

   Online clustering is analogous to categorizing a group of things as they arrive. It's useful for quickly organizing data.

   An online news aggregator, for example, employs online clustering to categorize and recommend articles as they are released.

# Case Studies

These approaches have found use in a variety of fields, including

1. **Healthcare Distributed Training**: Developing large-scale medical imaging models for disorders such as cancer or COVID-19

   Online learning: Using real-time clinical data to adapt predictive models for patient outcomes

2. **Finance Distributed Training**: Using distributed computing to train complicated risk assessment models for faster and more accurate forecasts

   Online learning: The process of constantly updating fraud detection algorithms to discover new fraudulent trends in financial transactions

3. **Distributed Training for Autonomous Vehicles**: Collaboratively training self-driving car models on data from several vehicles to increase safety and performance

   Online learning: Real-time adaptation to changing road conditions and traffic patterns

4. **Distributed Ecommerce Training**: Recommender systems that offer personalized product recommendations based on a large product catalog and user data

   Online learning: Updating inventory management models as new products are added or customer preferences change

Building scalable AI systems that can handle enormous datasets and respond to changing information requires distributed training techniques and online learning approaches. These strategies enable AI models to learn more quickly, make better decisions, and stay current in dynamic contexts.

As AI evolves, mastering these strategies will become increasingly important for AI practitioners, allowing them to create AI systems that can learn and adapt in the real world.

# Understanding Model Parallelism

Assume you have a massive puzzle that will not fit on a single table. To solve it, you must work on different areas of the puzzle on multiple tables at the same time. This is similar to how model parallelism works.

Model parallelism is an AI strategy that entails dividing a large neural network (a model) into smaller chunks or layers and running each component on a separate computer or accelerator (such as a GPU or TPU). These machines work together to do computations and make predictions.

# Why Model Parallelism Matters for Scalability

### Working with Large Models

AI models, particularly deep learning models, are getting huge. These models contain billions of parameters, and properly training them necessitates dividing the task over several devices or processors.

GPT-3, a well-known language model, has 175 billion parameters. It would be impractical to train it on a single machine.

### Managing Big Data

Many AI applications involve dealing with massive datasets. Model parallelism allows you to efficiently process these huge datasets.

For instance, training an AI model to recognize objects in satellite photos necessitates the processing of massive amounts of image data.

### Quicker Training

Parallelism can accelerate AI model training, making experimentation and research more efficient.

Training a model to play sophisticated games such as *Dota 2* or *StarCraft* can take a long time, but model parallelism allows it to be done faster.

# Practices and Strategies for Model Parallelism

1. **Model Parallelism vs. Data Parallelism**

   Splitting the dataset across numerous devices and executing the same model on each device is what data parallelism entails. This is appropriate when you have a large dataset but a model that can fit on a single device.

   Model parallelism, as previously said, divides the model into chunks and runs them on separate machines. When your model is too large for a single device, this is critical.

   For example, because the model itself is massive, you would normally use model parallelism while training a huge language model like GPT-3.

2. **Pipeline**

   Pipelining is a method of connecting many model parallelism steps. Before sending the computation to the next stage, each stage handles a portion of it. This keeps the devices occupied and cuts down on idle time.

   In an image processing pipeline, for example, one step may handle image recognition while the next stage detects objects.

3. **Distributed Training**

   Distributed training entails training a model on several machines, each accountable for a chunk of the data. Collectively, these devices interact and update the parameters of the model.

   For example, when training a recommendation system, each machine may handle a certain category of products (e.g., electronics, apparel) to learn consumer preferences.

4. **Gradient Accumulation**

   Due to memory limits, it may not be possible to fit the full model on a single device in some circumstances. Gradient accumulation is an approach that involves accumulating gradients over mini-batches before updating the model. This minimizes the amount of RAM used.

   For example, when training big image models, such as those used in computer vision, gradient accumulation can permit training on GPUs with limited memory.

5. **Model Sharding**

   Model sharding entails breaking down the model's parameters into smaller groups and assigning each group to a different device. This can assist in alleviating memory constraints.

   For example, while training a neural network for voice recognition, you may partition the model to process different frequencies of audio data on different devices.

# Advanced Techniques for Model Parallelism

1. **Mixed Precision Training**

   Mixed precision training involves training with both 16-bit and 32-bit floating-point integers. This saves memory while retaining model correctness.

   For example, developing a big image classification model with mixed precision training can dramatically reduce memory requirements.

2. **Gradient Checkpointing**

   Gradient checkpointing is a technique that recomputes intermediate activations of the model during backpropagation to save memory. This is especially handy for models with a large memory footprint.

   Checkpointing, for example, can enable you to train deeper networks without running out of memory while training deep reinforcement learning models.

**Elastic Inference**

Elastic inference is a service offered by cloud companies such as AWS that allows you to apply GPU acceleration to your instances on demand. This enables you to scale your model parallelism without having to manage GPU resources manually.

For example, if your AI application suffers sudden surges in demand, elastic inference helps ensure you have enough GPU resources without over-provisioning.

**Model Parallel Libraries**

Megatron and DeepSpeed are two libraries and frameworks that aim to make model parallelism easier. These solutions offer pre-implemented model parallelism strategies and can considerably simplify the complexity of scaling up AI models.

For instance, researchers and engineers can utilize DeepSpeed to rapidly train huge language models without delving into the complexities of model parallelism.

Model parallelism is a crucial scaling method in AI systems. It enables us to manage massive models and vast amounts of data while also speeding up training, making AI research and applications more accessible and efficient. We can harness the power of model parallelism to tackle complex AI problems and push the frontiers of what's possible in the realm of artificial intelligence by employing practices, tactics, and sophisticated approaches.

In this chapter, we covered the fundamental aspects of AI, emphasizing the role of algorithms and models. We explored scalable AI's ability to handle diverse tasks, from training models to making predictions and expanding capabilities. The discussion included distributed algorithms, model compression, distillation, ensemble learning, and various types of scalable AI models, such as neural networks and decision trees. The future of scalable AI involves democratization, explainable AI, AI in creativity and education, and distributed training techniques like parallelism and online learning. The case studies illustrated applications in healthcare, finance, autonomous vehicles, and ecommerce. Understanding model parallelism, its practices, and advanced techniques is crucial for managing large models efficiently. The conclusion highlights the significance of distributed training and model parallelism for building scalable AI systems capable of adapting in real-world scenarios.

# CHAPTER 5

# Scalable AI Infrastructure and Architecture

Assume you're constructing a house. You begin with a small, cozy cabin but expect your family to grow. As a result, you plan the foundation, plumbing, and electrical systems with future growth in mind. As a result, even if you add extra rooms or stories, your house will remain robust and functional. A similar notion underpins scalable AI infrastructure.

## The Foundation of Scalable AI

In the AI industry, scalability refers to the ability to develop and adapt without breaking down. It's about being able to handle more data, more sophisticated tasks, and more users without crumbling like a Jenga tower.

The underlying technology and software that allows AI systems to function is referred to as infrastructure. Scalable AI infrastructure, like a house's foundation, enables the AI applications we use every day.

Example 1: Cloud computing

Consider cloud computing to be a large, rentable computer playground. Companies such as Amazon, Google, and Microsoft provide these playgrounds, allowing enterprises to grow their AI projects. Instead of purchasing and maintaining real servers, they can rent processing power as needed.

Example 2: GPUs (Graphics Processing Units)

GPUs are the AI powerhouse. They excel at processing the complex mathematical computations required by AI. When training a larger AI model, a scalable AI infrastructure may require the use of additional GPUs. It's the same as adding additional engines to a rocket to carry a greater payload.

© Abhishek Mishra 2024
A. Mishra, *Scalable AI and Design Patterns*, https://doi.org/10.1007/979-8-8688-0158-7_5

Now, picture your house again. It's not just about having a strong foundation; it's also about how the rooms are connected, the flow of light and air, and where everything fits. Similarly, scalable AI architecture is about designing how AI components work together efficiently and effectively.

# Building Blocks of Scalable AI Architecture

**Components**: These are analogous to the rooms of your home. They can be AI models, databases, servers, or any other component of the AI system.

**Connectivity**: Just as hallways connect rooms, connectivity in AI design ensures that different components may communicate with each other. This is essential for data sharing and collaboration.

Consider yourself to be the architect of a self-driving car. Sensors (such as cameras and radar), a decision-making module (the car's "brain"), and the vehicle's control systems (steering, brakes, and so on) are among the components. The data flow between these components is defined as connectivity: sensors supply data to the decision module, which then transmits commands to the control systems.

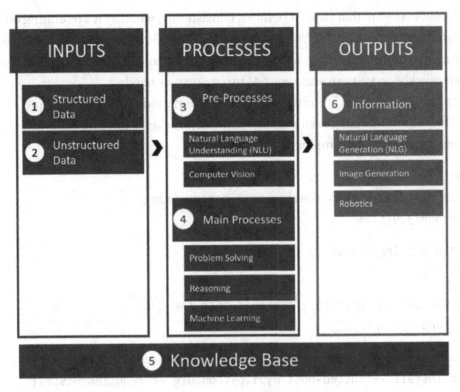

*Figure 5-1.* *Six steps which are critical building blocks for an AI system.*
*Reference:* www.researchgate.net/figure/Building-blocks-of-artificial-
intelligence-systems_fig1_337550604. *Image reference: Jan Kietzmann*

# Containerization and Orchestration for Scalability

What exactly is containerization?

Consider containerization to be a method of putting everything your AI system needs to run into a nice, portable box. These boxes are referred to as containers, and they include your AI code, libraries, dependencies, and even the environment in which your AI will operate.

Why should you containerize?

Assume you're sending a gift. You place it in a durable, standardized box to protect it and make transportation easier. Containerization has the same effect on your AI.

Containers ensure that your AI behaves consistently, whether it's operating on your laptop or in a large data center. You can move your containerized AI system from one environment to another without fear of incompatibility, and containers are lightweight and start quickly, so you can scale your AI up or down as needed.

Let's say you've built a fantastic image recognition model using Python and TensorFlow. Containerizing is straightforward with Docker, a popular containerization tool. Here's a simplified example:

```
# Dockerfile
# Use an official Python runtime as a parent image
FROM python:3.9-slim

# Set the working directory to /app
WORKDIR /app

# Copy the current directory contents into the container at /app
COPY . /app

# Install any needed packages specified in requirements.txt
RUN pip install --trusted-host pypi.python.org -r requirements.txt

# Make port 80 available to the world outside this container
EXPOSE 80

# Define environment variable
ENV NAME World

# Run app.py when the container launches
CMD ["python", "app.py"]
```

In this Dockerfile, you specify what your AI system needs (Python, dependencies, and how to run it). Once built into a container, you can ship it anywhere, and it will run consistently.

## Microservices Architecture

Microservices entail breaking down your AI program into discrete, autonomous services that can each run in their container. This technique has various advantages.

Individual services can be scaled independently. If one portion of your AI system requires additional computational power, you can allocate more containers to that service without affecting the others.

Fault isolation: If one microservice fails or suffers problems, it does not bring down the entire AI system. This separation improves the system's reliability.

Easier maintenance: Updating or adding new features becomes easier. Individual containers can be changed or replaced without affecting the overall system.

For example, in a natural language processing (NLP) application, you might have different microservices for text analysis, sentiment analysis, and translation.

## Container Orchestration Tools

While Docker is one of the most popular containerization tools, other solutions like Podman, containers, and rkt are available. Choosing the right tool depends on your specific requirements and infrastructure.

Advanced technique: Using Podman, you can create and manage containers without a daemon, which can be advantageous for security and compatibility in certain environments.

# Orchestration: Managing Containers at Scale

Orchestration is analogous to conducting a container orchestra. It ensures that all of your containers, whether five or five thousand, work in harmony. Orchestration technologies aid in tasks such as container deployment, scaling up or down, and load balancing.

Consider the difficulty of manually managing hundreds of containers. It's like attempting to conduct hundreds of musical instruments at the same time without a conductor. Orchestration overcomes this by doing the following:

> **Efficiency**: It saves time and reduces human error by automating many activities.

> **Scalability**: It refers to the ease with which containers can be added or removed to accommodate fluctuations in demand.

> **Reliability**: It is ensured by orchestration tools, which ensure that if a container fails, a new one is automatically launched in its place.

Kubernetes is a popular orchestration tool. Let's see how it can manage AI containers:

```
apiVersion: apps/v1
kind: Deployment
metadata:
  name: ai-model
spec:
  replicas: 3
  selector:
    matchLabels:
      app: ai-model
  template:
    metadata:
      labels:
        app: ai-model
    spec:
      containers:
      - name: ai-container
        image: your-ai-image:latest
        ports:
        - containerPort: 80
```

In this Kubernetes YAML file, you define a deployment with three replicas of your AI container. Kubernetes will ensure that three instances of your AI are always running, and if one fails, it'll replace it.

Affinity and advanced scheduling in Kubernetes has advanced scheduling tools that allow you to designate where containers should run. You may direct where your AI containers are deployed by using node affinity and pod affinity/anti-affinity policies.

Advanced technique: You can configure node affinity to execute AI containers on nodes that have certain hardware accelerators, like GPUs, which optimize performance for AI workloads.

```
affinity:
  nodeAffinity:
    requiredDuringSchedulingIgnoredDuringExecution:
      nodeSelectorTerms:
```

```
- matchExpressions:
   - key: ai-accelerator
     operator: In
     values:
       - gpu
```

StatefulSets for Persistent Storage

While many AI workloads are stateless, some, such as database containers or models that need to preserve checkpoints, require persistent storage.

Kubernetes StatefulSets are advanced techniques for managing stateful applications. They ensure that each container has a solid, unique network identity as well as persistent storage.

Use case: Deeper insights

# Advanced Personalization of Content Recommendation

Advanced personalization in content recommendation systems entails training separate models for each user. Containerization enables you to efficiently manage and grow these user-specific models.

For example, you can offer tailored content to millions of consumers by containerizing personalized recommendation models and orchestrating them with Kubernetes.

Federated learning for privacy-preserving AI use case: Federated learning is a sophisticated AI technology that lets several devices work together to develop a shared model while keeping data localized. Containers and orchestration can help to make federated learning systems easier to manage.

As an illustration, each participating device, such as a smartphone, runs a containerized federated learning agent. Kubernetes orchestrates these agents, ensuring that models are updated collaboratively without the need for sensitive data to be centralized.

Containerization and orchestration are the keys to unlocking the full potential of scalable AI systems, which are at the forefront of technology. You can design and manage scalable AI systems that are both efficient and dependable by using advanced containerization techniques, harnessing the power of microservices, and utilizing Kubernetes' advanced features.

# Resource Management for Scalable AI and Auto-Scaling Strategies

In the context of AI, resource management is like having a chef in a busy kitchen. To prepare meals efficiently, the chef requires materials, tools, and space. Similarly, AI systems require computing power, data, and memory to work well.

Resource management is the art of efficiently allocating and utilizing these resources to guarantee your AI applications work optimally.

As an example, consider data storage.

Assume you're developing an AI-powered ecommerce platform. To recommend products to consumers, large volumes of data, such as user profiles and product catalogs, must be stored and accessed. Resource management ensures that this data is efficiently kept and easily accessible.

# Best Practices for Resource Management

Now, let's look at some core recommended practices for managing resources successfully in scaled AI systems.

**Scalable Hardware**

Consider your AI system as an automobile. More passengers (data and duties) necessitate a larger car (hardware).

Best practice 1: Upgrade hardware. Check your hardware requirements regularly. If you discover your AI jobs are slowing down or you're running out of storage capacity, consider updating your hardware, such as adding more powerful GPUs or expanding RAM.

Example 1: GPU upgrade

If your AI model training is taking too long on your present GPU, upgrading to a more powerful one can substantially speed up the process.

**Load Balancing**

In our symphony analogy, load balancing is analogous to sharing the burden evenly among performers to achieve a harmonious performance.

Best practice 2: Utilize load balancers. When you have several servers or nodes, utilize load balancers to evenly distribute incoming AI jobs. This ensures that no single server is overburdened while others are underutilized.

Example 2: Web servers

A load balancer can route user requests to different web servers. This prevents any one server from receiving too many requests, resulting in a more seamless user experience.

### Elastic Scaling

Elasticity in resource management means that your AI system may expand or contract as needed, similar to how an accordionist adapts their instrument for different tunes.

Best practice 3: Use auto-scaling. Set up auto-scaling for your AI infrastructure. When demand increases, such as during a surge in users or data volume, auto-scaling automatically adds new resources. When demand falls, it scales down to save money.

Example 3: Cloud-based applications

Apps hosted in the cloud can automatically deploy extra virtual servers when traffic spikes (such as during a popular event) and lower them when the event is over.

### Containerization

Containers are like carefully filled lunchboxes. They contain everything an AI application requires, making it simple to move, replicate, and maintain.

Advanced technique 1: Container orchestration. Tools like Kubernetes manage containers efficiently, autonomously spreading them among servers as needed.

Example 4: Kubernetes in AI

Kubernetes can automatically deploy and manage containers running AI models, ensuring high availability and effective resource utilization.

### Serverless Computing

It's like hiring a chef who cooks food on demand. You don't have to worry about the kitchen or the ingredients; you merely pay for the dishes you want.

Advanced technique 2: Serverless AI. Services such as AWS Lambda and Azure Functions enable you to run AI functions without having to manage servers. They automatically assign resources and bill based on usage.

Let's see how these resource management strategies and advanced techniques work in real-life scenarios.

### Streaming Services

Imagine you're in charge of a popular streaming service. During major events, like the release of a blockbuster show, millions of users flock to your platform. Without efficient resource management, your service might crash.

Use case 1: Load balancing and auto-scaling

You employ load balancers to evenly distribute user requests to different servers. When the number of users spikes, auto-scaling kicks in, adding more servers to handle the load. When the hype dies down, servers are automatically scaled down to save costs.

**Autonomous Vehicles**

Autonomous vehicles are like AI-powered supercomputers on wheels. They constantly process data from sensors and cameras, making split-second decisions.

Use case 2: Containerization and container orchestration

AI components in autonomous vehicles are containerized, making them easy to manage and update. Container orchestration ensures these containers run smoothly and are distributed across the vehicle's hardware efficiently.

# Auto-Scaling Strategies for Scalable AI

Consider a magical bookshelf that extends to store as many books as you require. In the area of scalable AI, auto-scaling is analogous to the magical bookshelf. It enables AI systems to expand and contract in response to demand without the need for manual intervention.

Auto-scaling is analogous to having an AI system that can magically create more resources when needed and remove them when not. It's an important aspect of resource management since it keeps your AI system from becoming overburdened or wasting resources when they're not needed.

## The Need for Auto-Scaling

Consider owning a popular food truck. There's a queue around the block on a bright Saturday, and you need more ingredients, more personnel, and more space to service your customers. On a wet weekday, though, the queue is short, and you don't require all of those extra resources. Auto-scaling is analogous to having a food truck that can expand and decrease in response to the amount of hungry customers, and it works like setting up rules and triggers that instruct your AI system when to add or remove resources is what auto-scaling entails. These rules are similar to the directions you would give to your magical bookshelf: "Add a new shelf when there are more than 100 books." "Remove one when there are fewer than 50."

# Auto-Scaling Strategies

Now, let's delve into some common auto-scaling strategies used in scalable AI systems.

**Reactive Scaling**

It's like having a smart thermostat in your house. It responds to temperature changes by adjusting the heating or cooling.

Strategy 1: Threshold-based scaling

AI allows you to define thresholds that initiate auto-scaling. If the CPU usage approaches 80%, for example, the system immediately adds more computer resources.

Example 1: Auto-scaling on a web server

During a flash sale, a website's traffic suddenly increases. Threshold-based scaling detects rising demand and deploys more servers to accommodate it. Excess servers are withdrawn once the sale is over.

**Proactive Scaling**

Proactive scaling is analogous to having a weather app that predicts temperature changes. It predicts future demands and plans ahead of time.

Strategy 2: Predictive scaling

Predictive scaling anticipates resource requirements by using historical data and AI algorithms. If it forecasts a traffic spike during certain hours based on previous usage trends, it prescales resources accordingly.

Example 2: Predictive scaling in ecommerce

An ecommerce software analyzes shopping behavior and forecasts that Sundays will see the biggest traffic. It prescales resources on Sundays to ensure smooth performance without waiting for a spike.

**Scheduled Scaling**

Scaling on a schedule is similar to setting an alarm to wake up at a specified time. You anticipate when you will require additional resources.

Strategy 3: Time-based scaling

In other circumstances, such as a weekly data processing job, you know exactly when you'll have higher demand. You program auto-scaling to happen at specified times.

Example 3: Time-based scaling in batch processing

Every Saturday, a data analytics firm arranges a resource-intensive data processing assignment. On Saturdays, auto-scaling is set to contribute extra computer resources, ensuring the operation is completed fast.

### Machine Learning–Driven Scaling

Consider your thermostat can learn your preferences and predict your needs in addition to reacting to temperature changes.

Advanced technique 1: Machine learning–driven scaling

Machine learning in AI systems may analyze complicated patterns in resource utilization and make dynamic scaling decisions without using predefined thresholds.

Example 4: Machine learning–driven cloud resources

Machine learning is used by cloud providers to analyze the behavior of virtual machines and automatically modify resources based on projected traffic patterns.

### Hysteresis Scaling

Setting a high and low temperature for your thermostat is analogous to hysteresis scaling. When values fluctuate near a threshold, it prevents quick and wasteful scaling.

Hysteresis scaling is an advanced technique.

Hysteresis in AI auto-scaling entails setting a lower threshold for scaling down and an upper threshold for scaling up. This eliminates the need for regular, small-scale modifications.

Example 5: Cloud resource hysteresis

A cloud service uses hysteresis scaling to prevent repeatedly adding and deleting servers in response to traffic changes, hence lowering resource provisioning costs.

### Predictive Anomaly Detection

Predictive anomaly detection is analogous to having a smoke detector that not only sounds an alarm when it detects smoke but also forecasts when a fire will break out.

Predictive anomaly detection is the third advanced technique.

Predictive anomaly detection in AI auto-scaling employs AI algorithms to detect aberrant resource utilization patterns before they become significant. Scaling is triggered proactively.

Example 6: Detecting predictive anomalies in serverless computing

Predictive anomaly detection is used by serverless platforms to discover possible resource constraints before they cause performance concerns, facilitating smooth operation.

### Edge Computing and Auto-Scaling

To handle resource limits efficiently, edge computing, which brings AI computation closer to where it's needed, will rely largely on auto-scaling.

Future trend 1: Edge auto-scaling

AI systems at the edge, such as those found in IoT devices or self-driving drones, will dynamically alter resources to meet real-time demands.

### Serverless and Auto-Scaling Integration

With smooth auto-scaling embedded into the core of serverless systems, serverless computing will become even more widespread.

Future trend 2: Serverless native auto-scaling

Serverless platforms will include native auto-scaling features with little configuration, making them more accessible to a wider spectrum of developers.

Let's see how these auto-scaling strategies and advanced techniques function in practical scenarios.

### AI Services on the Cloud

Assume you're in charge of a cloud-based AI service that provides voice recognition. Workloads fluctuate throughout the day, with peaks occurring during business hours.

Application: Machine learning–driven scaling

Machine learning–driven scaling examines historical usage trends to forecast peak demand for speech recognition systems. It modifies resource allocation automatically to match projected surges in use.

### Drone Fleet on Autopilot

Autonomous drones are outfitted with artificial intelligence algorithms that process sensor data for navigation. The resource requirements of these drones vary greatly depending on the complexity of the terrain they explore.

Predictive scaling for autonomous drones is an example of a use case.

Drones use predictive scaling to analyze anticipated flight routes, detect places with difficult terrain, and deploy additional computing resources proactively to ensure smooth and safe navigation.

In the symphony of scalable AI, auto-scaling is the conductor's baton. It ensures that resources are allocated precisely when they are required, hence optimizing performance and cost-efficiency. Auto-scaling enables AI systems to adjust flexibly to changing needs by using methodologies ranging from reactive to predictive, as well as advanced techniques such as machine learning–driven scaling. As technology evolves and new trends arise, auto-scaling will remain an important tool in the armory of scalable AI, ensuring that AI systems always give their optimum performance when it is most needed.

Scalable AI infrastructure and architecture focus on constructing a foundation that accommodates growth in AI systems. Scalable infrastructure, akin to a house's foundation, supports AI applications. Cloud computing and GPUs are examples, allowing flexible expansion. Scalable AI architecture involves designing efficient AI component interactions. Components (e.g., models, databases) and connectivity (data sharing) are essential. Containerization encapsulates AI systems for consistency and portability. Microservices break down AI into autonomous services, aiding scalability, fault isolation, and maintenance. Container orchestration, exemplified by Kubernetes, efficiently manages containers at scale. StatefulSets in Kubernetes address persistent storage needs.

Resource management for scalable AI covers efficient allocation of computing resources. Best practices include upgrading hardware, load balancing for even task distribution, and elasticity through auto-scaling. Containerization, exemplified by Docker and Kubernetes, enhances resource efficiency. Serverless computing automates resource allocation based on demand. Use cases illustrate resource management strategies in scenarios like streaming services and autonomous vehicles.

Auto-scaling strategies for scalable AI explore auto-scaling as a key resource management aspect. Reactive scaling responds to immediate needs, while proactive scaling anticipates future demands. Scheduled scaling adjusts resources at predetermined times. Machine learning–driven scaling analyzes usage patterns for dynamic decisions. Hysteresis scaling prevents rapid, wasteful adjustments. Predictive anomaly detection identifies potential issues before they impact performance. Future trends include edge auto-scaling for real-time adjustments and serverless native auto-scaling for accessibility.

The chapter emphasizes auto-scaling as a crucial tool in optimizing AI system performance and cost-efficiency, adapting to changing needs through various methodologies and advanced techniques.

# CHAPTER 6

# Scalable AI Deployment and Productionization

Scalable AI deployment and productionization are all about bringing artificial intelligence's enormous potential into practice. It's like owning a powerful race vehicle but needing to ensure it operates properly on different circuits.

Assume you've constructed an AI that can accurately predict the weather. That's amazing, but it's not very useful if it just works on your computer. Scalable AI deployment is the process of taking that AI, packaging it, and making it available to a large number of individuals all over the world.

## Why Is Scalable AI Deployment Important?

Scalable deployment is the process of converting a creative idea into a product that can benefit a large number of people. It's not just about developing AI; it's about making it widely available and helpful. Assume you've created an AI that can diagnose diseases based on medical scans. Because of its scalability, this AI can assist doctors all over the world in making more accurate diagnoses, potentially saving lives.

Here are the top **five reasons** why scalable AI deployment is critically important:

- Scalable AI systems utilize computational resources efficiently, resulting in cost savings. They can automatically assign resources as needed, preventing over-provisioning and waste.

- **Handling Increased Workloads**: As AI applications grow in popularity, scalable deployment ensures that systems can handle bigger workloads. This is critical for services that encounter rapid surges in demand, such as online shopping during the holiday season.

© Abhishek Mishra 2024
A. Mishra, *Scalable AI and Design Patterns*, https://doi.org/10.1007/979-8-8688-0158-7_6

- Scalable AI moves AI from the lab to real-world applications. AI must tackle complicated problems and make a difference in industries such as healthcare, banking, and manufacturing.

- **Improved User Experience**: Scalable AI delivers consistent and smooth user experiences, even during peak usage. Users expect responsive and dependable services, and scalability assists in meeting these expectations.

- **Competitive Advantage**: Organizations that scale AI acquire a competitive advantage. They can develop faster, produce better products and services, and adapt to market changes more effectively, distinguishing themselves from the competition.

# Model Versioning and Deployment Strategies

Assume you're a chef in charge of a popular restaurant. Let's say your hallmark dish is a fantastic pasta carbonara that everyone loves. However, you're continuously thinking of ways to improve it. You occasionally try out new ingredients or cooking techniques. This iterative process of refining and upgrading your dish is analogous to the development and deployment of AI models. Model versioning and deployment strategies are the recipes and approaches that allow you to provide your customers with the best AI solutions.

We'll delve into the practices and strategies that underpin scalable AI systems, explaining them in straightforward terms and providing real-world examples.

## Why Is Model Versioning Important?

Assume you're writing a book and constantly modifying it to improve it. You wouldn't want to lose all of your past drafts, would you? Model versioning is analogous to preserving various drafts of your AI model. It helps you to keep track of changes, experiment with new features, and revert to a previous version if necessary.

# Best Practices for Model Versioning

1. **Version Control Systems (VCS)**: Use tools like Git to track changes in the code and configuration files of your AI model. This ensures that you have a historical record of all modifications and can effectively cooperate with a team.

   For instance, under your AI project folder, you execute git init to activate version control. Then, with informative commit messages, you use git commit to save the changes.

2. **Semantic Versioning**: Use a clear versioning scheme, such as "Major.Minor.Patch" (e.g., 1.0.2). Increase the version number based on the relevance of the changes. Major refers to major changes, Minor to new features, and Patch to bug fixes.

   For instance, if you improve the accuracy of your image recognition model, you might upgrade from 1.0.0 to 1.1.0.

3. **Supporting Documentation**: Maintain records for each model version. Describe the modifications, enhancements, and any potential impact on performance.

   For instance, in your project's README file, you include a section for version history and a description of what's new in each release.

4. **Testing and Validation**: Thoroughly test a new model version before deploying it to guarantee it outperforms the prior one. Validation guarantees that adjustments result in advancements.

   For example, suppose you train a new version of your chatbot model and test it against real-world user interactions to determine enhanced response accuracy.

# Deployment Strategies: Serving AI at Scale

Assume you've perfected your spaghetti carbonara recipe and are now launching a restaurant chain. You must ensure that every restaurant can prepare and serve your meal consistently, especially during peak hours. AI model deployment strategies ensure that your models can offer predictions consistently and efficiently, even at scale.

**Best Practices for Deployment Strategies**

1. **Rollout Deployment**

   What is it? Gradually introduce a new model version to a subset of users while keeping the old version active for others.

   Why use it? It reduces the risk of deploying a problematic model to all users at once.

   Example: In a music streaming app, you roll out a new recommendation model to 10% of users. If it performs well, you gradually increase its reach.

2. **Blue-Green Deployment**

   What is it? Maintain two identical environments: one for the current model version (blue) and one for the new version (green). Switch traffic to the new version when ready.

   Why use it? It ensures a seamless transition from old to new, with the ability to roll back quickly if issues arise.

   Example: In an ecommerce platform, you set up a new model version alongside the existing one. When the new version proves stable, you switch all user traffic to it.

3. **Canary Deployment**

   What is it? Similar to rollouts, you route a small portion of traffic to the new version to monitor its performance.

   Why use it? It allows real-time monitoring of how the new model behaves in production with limited user impact.

   Example: In a ride-sharing app, you send 5% of ride requests to a new routing model to ensure it optimizes routes without causing issues.

4. **A/B Testing**

   What is it? Compare the performance of two or more model versions by randomly assigning users to different groups exposed to different versions.

Why use it? It helps measure the impact of model changes on specific metrics like user engagement or conversion rates.

Example: In a news app, you show one group of users news recommendations from the old model and another group of recommendations from the new model to evaluate which performs better.

5. **Serverless Deployment**

   What is it? Deploy your AI model as a serverless function that automatically scales with demand.

   Why use it? It offers cost-effective scalability and ensures that you're not paying for idle resources.

   Example: In a chat application, you deploy a language translation model as a serverless function that translates messages on the fly.

6. **Continuous Integration/Continuous Deployment (CI/CD)**

   What is it? Automate the testing, building, and deployment of AI models whenever changes are made to the code or configuration.

   Why use it? It speeds up the deployment pipeline, reducing manual errors and ensuring rapid model updates.

   Example: Your AI project is set up with Jenkins, a CI/CD tool, to automatically test and deploy new model versions to production when changes are committed to the repository.

7. **Multi-model Deployment**

   What is it? Deploy multiple versions of a model simultaneously and route requests to the version that best suits each specific prediction.

   Why use it? It allows you to take advantage of different model strengths for different tasks, improving overall accuracy.

   Example: In a language translation service, you deploy multiple translation models and route requests based on language pairs, ensuring the best translation quality.

8. **Model Compression**

What is it? Reduce the size of AI models while preserving performance, making them more efficient to deploy and run.

Why use it? It enables faster inference and lowers resource requirements, especially useful for edge computing.

Example: You apply model quantization techniques to compress a large image recognition model, making it suitable for deployment on mobile devices.

The key components that transform AI models from experiments into practical solutions are model versioning and deployment methodologies. Organizations may serve AI solutions at scale while continuously increasing their quality and effectiveness by adhering to best practices, implementing deployment methods, and employing advanced approaches. These methods, like improving a prized recipe, necessitate care, documentation, and testing to assure success in the ever-changing world of AI.

# Monitoring and Performance Optimization for Scalable AI

Imagine you're driving a high-performance sports car on a long, winding road. To ensure a smooth and safe journey, you need to constantly monitor the car's performance, check for signs of wear and tear, and make adjustments when necessary. In the world of scalable AI, monitoring and performance optimization play a similar crucial role.

## Why Is Monitoring and Performance Optimization Important for Scalable AI?

Before diving into the strategies and techniques, let's understand why monitoring and performance optimization are so vital in the realm of scalable AI:

1. **Efficiency Matters**

Scalable AI systems often handle massive amounts of data and complex algorithms. Efficiency ensures that these systems operate smoothly without unnecessary resource consumption, reducing costs.

2. **Quality Assurance**

   Monitoring allows us to ensure that AI systems are performing as expected. It helps catch errors, anomalies, and issues early, preventing them from affecting users or business operations.

3. **Scaling Responsibly**

   As AI systems scale, they need to do so responsibly. Monitoring helps track resource utilization, preventing over-provisioning and ensuring that AI systems scale according to demand.

4. **Continuous Improvement**

   Performance optimization is about making AI systems smarter. By analyzing data and user interactions, we can fine-tune models and algorithms, making them more accurate and efficient over time.

# Practices and Strategies

Now, let's explore some fundamental practices and strategies for monitoring and performance optimization in scalable AI:

1. **Logging and Data Collection**

   Just as your car has a dashboard displaying essential information, AI systems have logs that record important events and metrics. These logs help monitor system health and performance.

   Practice 1: Comprehensive logging

   Ensure that your AI system logs relevant data, such as error messages, resource utilization, and user interactions. This data becomes invaluable for troubleshooting and performance analysis.

   Example: Logging in Python

   In Python, you can use libraries like "logging" to create detailed logs for your AI application.

```python
import logging
logging.basicConfig(filename='ai_system.log', level=logging.INFO)
logging.info('AI system started.')
```

2. **Real-Time Monitoring**

   Imagine having sensors in your car that constantly feed data to the dashboard. Real-time monitoring does the same for AI systems, providing instant insights into system behavior.

   Practice 2: Real-time dashboards

   Use tools like Grafana or Kibana to create real-time dashboards that display critical metrics like CPU usage, response times, and user traffic.

   Example: Real-time monitoring with Grafana

   Grafana allows you to build customizable dashboards that visualize data from various sources, providing real-time insights into system performance.

3. **Anomaly Detection**

   In your car, if the engine temperature suddenly spikes, you'd want an alert. Similarly, AI systems benefit from anomaly detection to identify unusual behavior.

   Practice 3: Anomaly detection algorithms

   Implement anomaly detection algorithms that can spot deviations from normal system behavior. For instance, you might use statistical methods or machine learning models.

   Example: Anomaly detection with Isolation Forest

   The Isolation Forest algorithm is used for anomaly detection. It can identify outliers in your data, which might indicate unusual behavior in your AI system.

```python
from sklearn.ensemble import IsolationForest

model = IsolationForest(contamination=0.05)
anomalies = model.fit_predict(data)
```

4. **Scalability Testing**

   Just as a car undergoes stress tests to ensure it performs under
   extreme conditions, AI systems should be tested for scalability.

   Practice 4: Load testing

   Simulate heavy loads on your AI system to see how it performs
   under stress. This helps identify bottlenecks and resource
   limitations.

   Example: Load testing with Apache JMeter

   Apache JMeter is a popular tool for load testing. It allows you to
   simulate multiple users making requests to your AI system to
   evaluate its performance under different loads.

5. **Continuous Integration and Deployment (CI/CD)**

   Your car gets regular maintenance to stay in peak condition.
   Similarly, AI systems benefit from a continuous integration and
   deployment pipeline.

   Practice 5: CI/CD pipeline

   Set up a CI/CD pipeline to automate the testing, deployment,
   and monitoring of changes to your AI system. This ensures that
   updates don't introduce performance regressions.

   Example: CI/CD with Jenkins

   Jenkins is a widely used tool for setting up CI/CD pipelines. It
   can automate the building, testing, and deployment of your AI
   application.

```groovy
pipeline {
    agent any

    stages {
        stage('Build') {
            steps {
                // Build your AI application here
            }
        }
        stage('Test') {
            steps {
                // Run tests on your AI system
            }
        }
        stage('Deploy') {
            steps {
                // Deploy the AI system to production
            }
        }
    }
}
```

Now, let's delve into some advanced techniques for monitoring and performance optimization in scalable AI systems:

1. **Auto-Scaling and Resource Orchestration**

   Auto-scaling, much like cruise control in a car, automatically adjusts resources to match demand, ensuring optimal performance and cost-efficiency.

   Advanced technique 1: Auto-scaling policies

   Implement auto-scaling policies that add or remove computing resources based on metrics like CPU utilization or user traffic.

   Example: AWS Auto Scaling

AWS Auto Scaling allows you to define scaling policies that automatically adjust the number of instances in an Amazon EC2 Auto Scaling group.

```json
{
    "scale_up_policy": {
        "metric_type": "CPUUtilization",
        "target_value": 70,
        "action": "add_instance"
    },
    "scale_down_policy": {
        "metric_type": "CPUUtilization",
        "target_value": 30,
        "action": "remove_instance"
    }
}
```

2.  **A/B Testing and Experimentation**

A/B testing is like trying different routes in your car to find the fastest one. In AI systems, it involves experimenting with different algorithms or models to see which performs best.

Advanced technique 2: A/B testing frameworks

Use A/B testing frameworks to run controlled experiments with different AI configurations and measure their impact on system performance.

Example: Split.io for A/B testing

Split.io is a platform that allows you to easily implement A/B tests in your AI applications to compare different models or algorithms.

```javascript
if (splitio.isTreatmentOn('new-model')) {
    // Use the new AI model
} else {
```

```
    // Use the existing model
}
```

3. **Reinforcement Learning for Optimization**

   Reinforcement learning is like having a car that learns from your driving habits. AI can optimize system behavior based on historical data.

   Advanced technique 3: Reinforcement learning controllers

   Implement reinforcement learning controllers that learn to make decisions that optimize system performance over time.

   Example: Reinforcement learning in resource allocation

   Reinforcement learning can be used to optimize resource allocation in a scalable AI system, dynamically adjusting resources based on changing workloads.

```python
# Reinforcement learning code example
```

# Real-World Use Cases

Let's explore real-world use cases where monitoring and performance optimization for scalable AI make a significant impact:

1. **Ecommerce Recommendation Systems**

   Imagine an ecommerce platform like Amazon. Their recommendation system uses AI to suggest products to users. Monitoring ensures that the recommendation engine is responsive, and performance optimization involves continually improving the accuracy of product recommendations to boost sales.

2. **Autonomous Vehicles**

   Autonomous vehicles rely on AI for navigation and decision-making. Real-time monitoring is critical for safety, and performance optimization involves fine-tuning algorithms to handle complex driving scenarios more effectively.

3. **Healthcare Diagnostics**

   In healthcare, AI is used to analyze medical images like X-rays and MRIs. Monitoring ensures that diagnostic systems provide timely results, and performance optimization focuses on increasing the accuracy of diagnoses.

   Just as a diligent driver keeps their car in top condition for a smooth ride, organizations must prioritize monitoring and performance optimization for their scalable AI systems. These practices and advanced techniques ensure that AI applications run efficiently, deliver high-quality results, and can adapt to evolving demands.

   By implementing comprehensive logging, real-time monitoring, anomaly detection, scalability testing, and CI/CD pipelines, organizations can maintain a high level of control over their AI systems. Additionally, advanced techniques like auto-scaling, A/B testing, and reinforcement learning allow organizations to optimize their AI systems for maximum efficiency and impact. In a world increasingly powered by AI, the ability to monitor and optimize scalable AI systems is not just a best practice; it's a strategic imperative. It enables organizations to deliver superior services, remain competitive, and drive innovation forward. Just like a well-maintained car delivers a fantastic driving experience, well-monitored and optimized AI systems can provide exceptional value and impact to businesses and society as a whole.

# Building Production-Grade AI Systems: Unleashing the Power of AI in the Real World

Artificial intelligence (AI) has evolved from a buzzword to a transformative force across various industries. We see AI-powered recommendations on ecommerce platforms, chatbots providing customer support, and autonomous vehicles navigating our streets. However, building AI is not just about developing smart algorithms; it's about creating robust and dependable systems that can handle real-world challenges.

# Understanding Production-Grade AI Systems

Imagine you're a chef. You've perfected your secret recipe for a delicious dish, but now you need to cook it consistently and quickly for hundreds of hungry customers. Production-grade AI systems are like the well-oiled kitchens in high-end restaurants—they take the chef's expertise and turn it into a reliable and efficient process that delivers the same exceptional quality every time.

Building production-grade AI systems is crucial for several reasons:

1. **Reliability**

   In a restaurant, consistency is key. Customers expect the same taste and quality with every order. Similarly, in AI systems, reliability is paramount. Whether it's diagnosing medical conditions or processing financial transactions, errors can have significant consequences. Production-grade systems ensure dependable performance.

2. **Scalability**

   Restaurants need to serve both a handful of diners and a full house. Likewise, AI systems must be able to handle varying workloads. Scalability ensures that as demand grows, the system can expand to meet it, whether it's serving ten users or ten million.

3. **Performance Optimization**

   Just as a chef optimizes cooking techniques, AI systems must be fine-tuned for performance. This includes reducing processing time, improving accuracy, and optimizing resource usage.

4. **Monitoring and Maintenance**

   Restaurants regularly inspect their kitchens and equipment
   to ensure they're in top shape. Similarly, AI systems require
   continuous monitoring to identify issues, fix bugs, and update
   models to keep them relevant.

5. **Security**

   In the restaurant industry, food safety is a priority. In AI systems,
   data security is paramount. Production-grade systems implement
   robust security measures to protect sensitive information and
   ensure compliance with data privacy regulations.

# Building Production-Grade AI: Techniques and Best Practices

Building production-grade AI systems involves a combination of techniques and best
practices. Let's explore these concepts with examples and code snippets:

1. **Code Modularity and Documentation**

   Technique 1: Code modularity

   In AI, complex models can be broken down into smaller,
   manageable components. This makes code more maintainable
   and allows teams to work on different parts simultaneously.

   Example: In a speech recognition AI system, you can have
   separate modules for audio preprocessing, feature extraction, and
   language modeling.

   ```python
   # Example of a modular code structure
   from audio_preprocessing import preprocess_audio
   from feature_extraction import extract_features
   from language_model import generate_text
   ```

```
audio_data = preprocess_audio(audio_input)
features = extract_features(audio_data)
transcription = generate_text(features)
```

Technique 2: Documentation

Comprehensive documentation ensures that developers and
stakeholders understand the codebase, making maintenance and
troubleshooting more accessible.

Example: Use comments and docstrings to explain the purpose
and functionality of functions and classes.

```python
# Function to preprocess audio data
def preprocess_audio(audio_input):
    """

    Preprocesses raw audio input.

    Args:
        audio_input (numpy.array): Raw audio data.

    Returns:
        numpy.array: Processed audio data.
    """

    # Preprocessing code here
    return processed_audio
```

2. **Automated Testing**

Technique 3: Unit testing

Unit tests verify that individual components of your AI system
work correctly. They catch bugs early and ensure that changes to
the code don't introduce new issues.

Example: Using the "unittest" library in Python to write a unit test
for the preprocessing function.

```python
import unittest
from audio_preprocessing import preprocess_audio

class TestAudioPreprocessing(unittest.TestCase):

    def test_preprocess_audio(self):
        # Test preprocessing function
        input_audio = [0.1, 0.2, 0.3]
        processed_audio = preprocess_audio(input_audio)
        self.assertEqual(len(processed_audio), 3)
```

Technique 4: Integration testing

Integration tests check how different components of your AI system work together. They ensure that the system functions correctly as a whole.

Example: An integration test that simulates the entire audio processing pipeline.

```python
import unittest
from audio_processing_pipeline import process_audio_pipeline

class TestAudioProcessingPipeline(unittest.TestCase):

    def test_audio_processing_pipeline(self):
        # Test the entire audio processing pipeline
        input_audio = [0.1, 0.2, 0.3]
        transcription = process_audio_pipeline(input_audio)
        self.assertTrue(transcription.startswith("The
        weather is"))
```

3. **Continuous Integration and Deployment (CI/CD)**

   Technique 5: CI/CD pipelines

   CI/CD pipelines automate the testing, building, and deployment of AI systems. They ensure that code changes are thoroughly tested and safely deployed to production.

   Example: Using a CI/CD tool like Jenkins or GitLab CI/CD to automate the testing and deployment process whenever code changes are pushed to a repository.

4. **Scalability and Performance Optimization**

   Technique 6: Distributed computing

   For AI systems that need to scale, distributed computing frameworks like Apache Spark or Kubernetes can be employed to distribute workloads across multiple machines.

   Example: Using Apache Spark to parallelize the processing of large datasets.

```python
from pyspark import SparkContext
sc = SparkContext("local", "wordcount")
data = ["Hello", "world", "this", "is", "a", "word", "count",
"example"]
rdd = sc.parallelize(data)
result = rdd.countByValue()

```

   Technique 7: Model optimization

   AI models can be optimized for performance by reducing their size or using hardware acceleration like GPUs or TPUs.

   Example: Optimizing a deep learning model for image classification using TensorFlow and GPU acceleration.

```python
import tensorflow as tf
```

```
# Load the pre-trained model
model = tf.keras.applications.MobileNetV2(weights='
imagenet')

# Optimize the model for inference on GPU
optimized_model = tf.function(model)
```

5. **Monitoring and Maintenance**

   Technique 8: Logging and monitoring

   Logging and monitoring tools like Prometheus or ELK Stack
   track the health and performance of AI systems in real time. They
   provide alerts for anomalies and help in diagnosing issues quickly.

   Example: Implementing logging to record system events and
   performance metrics.

```python
import logging
# Configure logging
logging.basicConfig(filename='ai_system.log', level=logging.INFO)

# Log an event
logging.info('Processing completed successfully)
```

   Technique 9: Automated error reporting

   Automated error reporting tools can notify developers of issues as
   they occur, enabling rapid response and resolution.

   Example: Integrating error reporting with a service like Sentry to
   receive real-time error alerts.

# Real-World Use Cases of Production-Grade AI Systems

Let's explore some real-world use cases where production-grade AI systems have made a
significant impact:

1.  **Healthcare Diagnosis**

    In healthcare, AI systems are used for diagnosing medical images such as X-rays and MRIs. Production-grade systems ensure that these AI models are reliable, secure, and capable of providing accurate diagnoses consistently.

2.  **Autonomous Vehicles**

    Autonomous vehicles rely on AI systems for navigation and decision-making. Building production-grade AI ensures that these vehicles can operate safely and efficiently in complex real-world environments.

3.  **Natural Language Processing (NLP) for Customer Support**

    Many companies use AI-powered chatbots for customer support. Production-grade AI systems guarantee that these chatbots can understand and respond to customer queries accurately and promptly.

Building production-grade AI systems is the key to unleashing the full potential of AI in the real world. It goes beyond developing intelligent algorithms and focuses on creating reliable, scalable, and efficient solutions that can make a meaningful impact across industries. By implementing techniques like code modularity, automated testing, CI/CD pipelines, scalability, and robust monitoring, organizations can build AI systems that are not just innovative but also dependable. As AI continues to shape the future, the ability to build production-grade AI systems will be a defining factor in driving progress and achieving transformative results in various domains.

**CHAPTER 7**

# Scalable AI for Real-Time and Streaming Data

The demand for real-time and streaming data processing has increased in the dynamic landscape of data-driven technology. Incorporating scalable artificial intelligence (AI) has become critical as organizations attempt to get actionable insights from fast-streaming data. Real-time data is information that is generated and analyzed instantly, allowing for quick decision-making. Live social media updates, sensor data from IoT devices, and financial market movements are some examples.

Streaming data is a continuous stream of information processed as it arrives. Unlike batch processing, which deals with data in pieces, streaming data is dealt with in real time. Live video broadcasts, website clickstream data, and real-time health monitoring are examples.

## The Need for Scalable AI in Real-Time and Streaming Data

Traditional data processing technologies are struggling to keep up with the increasing volume and velocity of data. Scalable AI tackles this issue by handling increasing workloads efficiently without sacrificing performance. Let's look at why scalability is important with real-time and streaming data.

Example: Ecommerce recommendations

Consider a real-time ecommerce platform that analyzes user behavior to deliver personalized product recommendations. A scalable AI system ensures that the recommendation engine can handle the rising data stream, offering instant suggestions without delays.

95

© Abhishek Mishra 2024
A. Mishra, *Scalable AI and Design Patterns*, https://doi.org/10.1007/979-8-8688-0158-7_7

# Challenges in Scalable AI for Real-Time and Streaming Data

While scalable AI offers immense benefits, certain challenges must be addressed to ensure effective implementation in real-time and streaming data scenarios.

1. **Latency**

   Latency refers to the delay between data generation and its processing. In real-time applications, low latency is crucial for timely decision-making.

   Example: Autonomous vehicles

   In the context of self-driving cars, a scalable AI system must minimize latency in processing sensor data to make split-second decisions. High latency could lead to delayed responses, posing safety risks.

2. **Resource Allocation**

   Efficient allocation of computing resources is essential for scalability. Inadequate resource management can result in performance bottlenecks.

   Example: Cloud-based scalable AI

   Consider a cloud-based scalable AI system for real-time language translation. Proper resource allocation ensures that the system can handle an increasing number of translation requests without compromising on speed and accuracy.

3. **Data Consistency**

   Maintaining consistency across distributed data sources is challenging. Inconsistent data can lead to inaccuracies in AI models.

   Example: Financial transactions

   In real-time financial data processing, a scalable AI system must ensure consistency across multiple transactions. Inconsistencies could lead to errors in fraud detection or financial analysis.

In this age of rapid technical developments, scalable AI for real-time and streaming data is a game changer. As several examples show, incorporating scalable AI enables systems to handle rising data quantities while assuring fast and intelligent processing. Organizations can exploit the full potential of scaled AI to generate actionable insights from the ever-expanding ocean of real-time and streaming data by understanding the major components, challenges, and best practices. The real-world applications in various industries demonstrate the transformative influence of scalable AI, paving the path for a future in which intelligent processing is associated with real-time efficiency.

# Handling High-Velocity Data in Real Time with Scalable AI Systems

In the fast-paced world of data, where information flows at unprecedented speeds, handling high-velocity data in real time has become a critical challenge. The integration of scalable AI systems is key to efficiently processing and deriving meaningful insights from this torrent of high-velocity data. Let's delve into practices, strategies, and advanced techniques that support the seamless handling of high-velocity data in real time using scalable AI systems. Let's break down the complexities into easy-to-understand components.

## Practices for Handling High-Velocity Data

1.  **Stream Processing**

    Stream processing involves the real-time analysis of data as it is generated. This practice is fundamental for handling high-velocity data streams efficiently.

    Example:

    Imagine a social media platform analyzing tweets in real time. Stream processing allows the platform to instantly identify trending topics and user sentiments as tweets are posted.

2. **In-Memory Computing**

In-memory computing stores and processes data in the system's main memory, eliminating the need to access data from disk storage. This significantly accelerates data processing speed.

Example:

Consider a financial trading system where stock prices are updated in real time. In-memory computing enables quick access to the latest stock prices, facilitating timely trading decisions.

# Strategies for Scalable AI Systems

1. **Parallelization**

Parallelization involves breaking down a task into smaller subtasks that can be executed simultaneously, maximizing computational efficiency.

Example:

In high-velocity data processing, a scalable AI system can use parallelization to analyze different segments of data streams concurrently, ensuring swift and accurate insights.

2. **Auto-Scaling**

Auto-scaling allows the AI system to dynamically adjust its computational resources based on the volume of incoming data, ensuring optimal performance during peak loads.

Example:

In an ecommerce platform handling high-velocity transaction data, auto-scaling ensures that the AI system seamlessly scales up or down to accommodate fluctuations in user activity.

# Advanced Techniques for High-Velocity Data Processing

1. **Approximate Computing**

   Approximate computing allowing a certain degree of error in computations to achieve faster processing speeds, which is particularly useful for real-time applications.

   Example:

   In video streaming services, approximate computing can be employed to quickly compress and transmit video data, providing a smoother streaming experience.

2. **Edge Computing**

   Edge computing involves processing data closer to the source (at the edge of the network) rather than relying solely on centralized cloud servers. This reduces latency in data processing.

   Example:

   In IoT devices collecting high-velocity sensor data, edge computing enables on-device AI analysis, reducing the time it takes to generate actionable insights.

# Use Cases: Real-World Applications

1. **Financial Fraud Detection**

   In the banking sector, a scalable AI system employing stream processing can detect potentially fraudulent transactions in real time. By analyzing transaction patterns instantly, it can trigger alerts or block suspicious activities before they escalate.

2. **Internet of Things (IoT)**

   In a smart city project, high-velocity data from various IoT devices, such as traffic sensors and environmental monitors, can be processed in real time. Scalable AI systems enable quick decision-making for efficient city management.

## Code Snippets: Implementing Scalable AI for High-Velocity Data

1. **Stream Processing with Apache Flink**

```python
from pyflink.datastream import StreamExecutionEnvironment
from pyflink.table import StreamTableEnvironment

# Set up the execution environment
env = StreamExecutionEnvironment.get_execution_environment()
t_env = StreamTableEnvironment.create(env)

# Define and process a data stream
t_env.execute_sql("""
    CREATE TABLE high_velocity_data (
        timestamp TIMESTAMP,
        value DOUBLE
    ) WITH (
        'connector' = 'kafka',
        'topic' = 'high_velocity_topic',
        'properties.bootstrap.servers' = 'kafka:9092',
        'format' = 'json'
    )
""")

result = t_env.execute_sql("""
    SELECT
        TUMBLE_START(timestamp, INTERVAL '1' SECOND) AS
        window_start,
        AVG(value) AS avg_value
    FROM high_velocity_data
    GROUP BY TUMBLE(timestamp, INTERVAL '1' SECOND)
""")
```

2.  **Auto-Scaling with Kubernetes**

```yaml
apiVersion: apps/v1
kind: Deployment
metadata:
  name: scalable-ai-deployment
spec:
  replicas: 3
  template:
    spec:
      containers:
      - name: scalable-ai-container
        image: scalable-ai-image
---
apiVersion: autoscaling/v2beta2
kind: HorizontalPodAutoscaler
metadata:
  name: scalable-ai-autoscaler
spec:
  scaleTargetRef:
    apiVersion: apps/v1
    kind: Deployment
    name: scalable-ai-deployment
  minReplicas: 3
  maxReplicas: 10
  metrics:
  - type: Resource
    resource:
      name: cpu
      targetAverageUtilization: 70
```

In this Kubernetes configuration, the deployment automatically scales based on CPU utilization, ensuring optimal resource allocation for handling high-velocity data.

Handling high-velocity data in real time is a demanding task, but with scalable AI systems and the right practices, strategies, and advanced techniques, it becomes an achievable feat. Real-world applications across various industries demonstrate the transformative impact of efficiently processing high-velocity data, providing organizations with timely insights and enabling data-driven decision-making in the era of rapid information flow. As technology continues to advance, the marriage of scalable AI and high-velocity data processing will play a pivotal role in shaping the future of real-time analytics and intelligent systems.

# Real-Time Inference Techniques for Scalable AI: Unleashing Advanced Practices

In the fast-paced landscape of artificial intelligence (AI), the demand for real-time inference capabilities is on the rise. As organizations strive to deploy scalable AI systems, the ability to make instant predictions and decisions becomes paramount. Let's delve into the practices and strategies that support real-time inference in scalable AI, exploring advanced techniques and use cases and providing examples or code snippets in an easy-to-understand language.

Real-time inference refers to the process of making predictions or decisions in real time based on input data.

In the context of AI, this involves deploying models to make instantaneous predictions without compromising accuracy. Scalable AI, in this context, focuses on ensuring that the inference process can handle a growing workload efficiently.

1. **Model Quantization**

   Model quantization involves reducing the precision of the numerical values in a model. This not only reduces the memory footprint of the model but also speeds up inference.

   Example:

   Consider a computer vision model for object detection. By quantizing the model, you can represent weights and activations using fewer bits, making the inference process faster, which is crucial for real-time applications.

Code snippet (Python—TensorFlow):

```python
import tensorflow as tf
converter = tf.lite.TFLiteConverter.from_saved_model(saved_
model_dir)
converter.optimizations = [tf.lite.Optimize.DEFAULT]
quantized_tflite_model = converter.convert()
```

2. **Model Pruning**

Model pruning involves removing unnecessary parameters
(weights and neurons) from a model, leading to a more compact
and efficient network.

Example:

In natural language processing, a language model can undergo
pruning to remove less important connections. The pruned model
retains high accuracy but is faster during inference.

Code snippet (Python—TensorFlow):

```python
import tensorflow as tf
pruned_model = tfmot.sparsity.keras.strip_pruning(model)
```

3. **Asynchronous Inference**

In asynchronous inference, multiple inference requests are
processed concurrently without waiting for the completion of
each request. This enhances throughput in scalable systems.

Example:

Imagine a recommendation system for an ecommerce platform.
Asynchronous inference enables the system to handle multiple
user requests simultaneously, providing instant product
recommendations.

Code snippet (Python—FastAPI):

```python
from fastapi import FastAPI
import asyncio

app = FastAPI()

async def async_inference(request_data):
    # Perform asynchronous inference here
    await asyncio.sleep(1)  # Simulating inference delay
    return {"result": "Inference complete"}

@app.post("/predict")
async def predict(request_data: dict):
    response = await async_inference(request_data)
    return response
```

# Strategies for Real-Time Inference

1. **Edge Computing**

   Edge computing involves processing data closer to the source of generation, reducing latency and enabling real-time inference at the edge devices.

   Example:

   In a smart camera system for security surveillance, edge computing allows the camera to perform real-time object detection without sending the entire video stream to a centralized server.

2. **Model Caching**

   Model caching involves storing intermediate results of previous inferences. If the same or similar input is encountered again, the cached result can be used instead of rerunning the inference, saving computation time.

Example:

In a chatbot application, if a user asks a frequently encountered question, model caching can be employed to provide an instant response without rerunning the entire natural language processing model.

Code snippet (Python—Flask):

```python
from flask import Flask, request, jsonify
from cachetools import cached, TTLCache

app = Flask(__name__)
cache = TTLCache(maxsize=100, ttl=300)  # Cache with a time-to-live of 300 seconds

@cached(cache)
def perform_inference(input_data):
    # Perform inference here
    return {"result": "Inference complete"}

@app.route('/predict', methods=['POST'])
def predict():
    request_data = request.get_json()
    response = perform_inference(request_data)
    return jsonify(response)
```

3. **Load Balancing**

Load balancing involves distributing inference requests across multiple servers or processing units, preventing bottlenecks and ensuring optimal resource utilization.

Example:

In a real-time image recognition system, load balancing ensures that incoming image classification requests are distributed evenly among available GPUs, maximizing throughput.

# Advanced Techniques for Scalable AI

1. **Ensemble Learning**

   Ensemble learning involves combining predictions from multiple models to enhance accuracy and robustness. This technique is particularly useful for real-time applications where diverse models contribute to the final decision.

   Example:

   In a fraud detection system, an ensemble of different machine learning models can be employed to analyze transaction data. The combined prediction provides a more reliable fraud detection mechanism.

   Code snippet (Python—scikit-learn):

```python
from sklearn.ensemble import VotingClassifier
from sklearn.model_selection import train_test_split
from sklearn.metrics import accuracy_score
from sklearn.linear_model import LogisticRegression
from sklearn.svm import SVC
from sklearn.ensemble import RandomForestClassifier

# Create individual models
model1 = LogisticRegression()
model2 = SVC()
model3 = RandomForestClassifier()

# Create an ensemble model
ensemble_model = VotingClassifier(estimators=[('lr', model1),
('svc', model2), ('rf', model3)], voting='hard')

# Train the ensemble model
ensemble_model.fit(X_train, y_train)

# Make predictions
predictions = ensemble_model.predict(X_test)
```

2. **Federated Learning**

Federated learning allows model training to occur across multiple
decentralized devices or servers without exchanging raw data.
This is particularly beneficial for real-time applications where
privacy is a concern.

Example:

In a healthcare scenario, where patient data is sensitive, federated
learning enables training a predictive model across various
hospitals without centralizing patient information.

Code snippet (Python—PySyft):

```python
import syft
import torch

# Create a PySyft hook
hook = syft.TorchHook(torch)

# Create virtual workers (simulating decentralized devices)
bob = syft.VirtualWorker(hook, id="bob")
alice = syft.VirtualWorker(hook, id="alice")

# Train a model using federated learning
model = torch.nn.Linear(2, 1)
optimizer = torch.optim.SGD(params=model.parameters(), lr=0.1)

for epoch in range(10):
    # Send the model to the virtual workers
    model = model.send(bob)

    # Perform local training on each worker
    bob_model = model.copy().send(bob)
    alice_model = model.copy().send(alice)

    bob_optimizer = torch.optim.SGD(params=bob_model.
    parameters(), lr=0.1)
    alice_optimizer = torch.optim.SGD(params=alice_model.
    parameters(), lr=0.1)
```

```
    # Local training on each worker
    for _ in range(5):
        bob_optimizer.zero_grad()
        bob_prediction = bob_model(X_bob)
        bob_loss = loss(bob_prediction, y_bob)
        bob_loss.backward()
        bob_optimizer.step()

        alice_optimizer.zero_grad
()
        alice_prediction = alice_model(X_alice)
        alice_loss = loss(alice_prediction, y_alice)
        alice_loss.backward()
        alice_optimizer.step()

    # Aggregate model updates
    with torch.no_grad():
        model.weight.set_(((bob_model.weight.data + alice_model.
        weight.data) / 2).get())
        model.bias.set_(((bob_model.bias.data + alice_model.bias.
        data) / 2).get())

    # Get the model back from the virtual workers
    model = model.get()
```

3. **Neural Architecture Search (NAS)**

NAS involves automating the process of designing neural network architectures, leading to models optimized for specific tasks. This technique is valuable for real-time applications where model efficiency is crucial.

Example:

In a real-time speech recognition system, NAS can be employed to automatically search for the most efficient neural network architecture, minimizing computational requirements while maintaining high accuracy.

Code snippet (Python—Keras Tuner):

```python
from kerastuner.tuners import RandomSearch
from kerastuner.engine.hyperparameters import HyperParameters
from tensorflow.keras.models import Sequential
from tensorflow.keras.layers import Dense

# Define the model-building function for NAS
def build_model(hp):
    model = Sequential()
    model.add(Dense(units=hp.Int('units', min_value=32, max_
    value=512, step=32), input_dim=8, activation='relu'))
    model.add(Dense(1, activation='sigmoid'))
    model.compile(optimizer='adam', loss='binary_crossentropy',
    metrics=['accuracy'])
    return model

# Instantiate the RandomSearch tuner
tuner = RandomSearch(
    build_model,
    objective='val_accuracy',
    max_trials=5,
    directory='nas',
    project_name='real_time_speech_recognition'
)

# Perform the search
tuner.search(x_train, y_train, epochs=5, validation_data=
(x_val, y_val))
```

# Real-World Use Cases

1. **Autonomous Vehicles**

   In autonomous vehicles, real-time inference is critical for decision-making. Techniques such as model quantization and edge computing enable onboard AI systems to process sensor data instantly, ensuring rapid response to changing road conditions.

2. **Healthcare Diagnostics**

   Real-time inference in healthcare diagnostics allows for quick analysis of medical images or patient data. Model caching can be employed to store previous diagnoses, speeding up the process of identifying potential health issues.

3. **Predictive Maintenance in Manufacturing**

   In manufacturing, real-time inference is applied to predict equipment failures. Load balancing ensures that multiple machines can be monitored simultaneously, optimizing the maintenance process and minimizing downtime.

Real-time inference in scalable AI systems is a frontier that continues to evolve with advancements in technology. The practices, strategies, and advanced techniques explored in this chapter provide a foundation for building efficient and responsive AI applications.

As demonstrated through examples and code snippets, the integration of these techniques into real-world scenarios is not only feasible but also crucial for meeting the demands of today's data-driven and fast-paced environments. By leveraging these practices, organizations can ensure that their AI systems not only scale with increasing workloads but also deliver timely and accurate predictions, laying the groundwork for a future where intelligent decision-making happens in the blink of an eye.

# Scalable AI for Real-Time Applications

In the fast-paced world of technology, the demand for real-time applications powered by artificial intelligence (AI) is skyrocketing. Businesses seek to harness the power of AI to make instant decisions and derive actionable insights from data streams. However, achieving scalability in AI for real-time applications presents its own set of challenges. We'll break down complex concepts into easy-to-understand explanations, providing examples and even delving into code snippets to illustrate key points.

Scalability in the context of AI for real-time applications refers to the system's ability to handle increased workloads efficiently. This involves not only accommodating growing amounts of data but also ensuring that the system remains responsive and performs well as demand fluctuates.

Consider a real-time language translation service. As the number of users requesting translations simultaneously increases, a scalable AI system ensures that response times remain low, maintaining a seamless user experience. Without scalability, the system might struggle to keep up with demand, leading to delays and potential service disruptions.

# Practices for Building Scalable AI Systems

1. **Parallel Processing**

   Parallel processing involves dividing a task into smaller subtasks that can be executed simultaneously, boosting overall performance.

   Example:

   Let's say we're building an AI system for real-time image recognition. By using parallel processing, we can split the image analysis task across multiple processors. Each processor works on a distinct section of the image, significantly speeding up the overall recognition process.

Code illustration (Python):

```python
from concurrent.futures import ProcessPoolExecutor

def process_image(image_section):
    # AI image processing logic
    return result

def parallel_image_processing(image):
    sections = split_image(image)

    with ProcessPoolExecutor() as executor:
        results = list(executor.map(process_image, sections))

    # Combine results and perform final processing
    final_result = combine_results(results)

    return final_result
```

2. **Distributed Computing**

   Distributed computing involves spreading computational tasks across multiple interconnected devices or servers, improving overall system efficiency.

   Example: Fraud detection in banking

   For real-time fraud detection in financial transactions, a scalable AI system can distribute the analysis of transaction patterns across a cluster of servers. This distributed approach enhances the system's ability to process a large number of transactions concurrently.

   Code illustration (Python):

```python
from dask import delayed, compute

def analyze_transaction(transaction):
    # AI fraud detection logic
    return result
```

```
transactions = get_real_time_transactions()

# Distributed computing using Dask
delayed_results = [delayed(analyze_transaction)(transaction) for
transaction in transactions]
final_results = compute(*delayed_results)
```

3. **Microservices Architecture**

   Microservices architecture involves breaking down an application into small, independent services that communicate with each other, promoting flexibility and scalability.

   Example: Ecommerce platform

   In a real-time ecommerce platform, different AI services, such as recommendation, inventory tracking, and user profiling, can be implemented as microservices. This modular approach allows each service to scale independently, contributing to overall system scalability.

   Code illustration (Node.js):

```javascript
// Sample microservice for recommendation
const express = require('express');
const app = express();

app.get('/recommend/:userId', (req, res) => {
    const userId = req.params.userId;
    // AI recommendation logic
    const recommendations = getRecommendations(userId);
    res.json(recommendations);
});
```

```
const port = 3000;
app.listen(port, () => {
    console.log(`Recommendation microservice listening at
    http://localhost:${port}`);
});
```

4. **Containerization**

Containerization involves encapsulating an application and its dependencies into a container, ensuring consistency across different environments.

Example: Natural language processing (NLP) service

For a real-time NLP service, containerization allows the AI model and its dependencies to be packaged together. This ensures that the NLP service runs consistently, whether deployed on a local machine or in a cloud environment.

Code illustration (Dockerfile):

```dockerfile
FROM python:3.8

# Set working directory
WORKDIR /app

# Copy application files
COPY requirements.txt .
COPY nlp_service.py .

# Install dependencies
RUN pip install --no-cache-dir -r requirements.txt

# Expose the service port
EXPOSE 5000

# Command to run the service
CMD ["python", "nlp_service.py"]
```

# Advanced Techniques for Scalable AI in Real-Time Applications

1.  **Asynchronous Processing**

    Asynchronous processing allows a system to continue handling requests while waiting for time-consuming tasks to complete, improving overall responsiveness.

    Example: Chatbot service

    For a real-time chatbot, asynchronous processing can be used to handle multiple user queries concurrently. While one query is being processed, the system can still accept and initiate processing for other incoming queries.

    Code illustration (Python—using FastAPI):

    ```python
    from fastapi import FastAPI
    import asyncio

    app = FastAPI()

    async def process_user_query(query):
        # AI chatbot logic
        await asyncio.sleep(5)  # Simulating time-consuming task
        return f"Response to: {query}"

    @app.post("/chat")
    async def chat_endpoint(query: str):
        result = await process_user_query(query)
        return {"response": result}
    ```

2.  **Auto-Scaling**

    Auto-scaling allows a system to automatically adjust its resources based on demand, ensuring optimal performance during peak usage.

Example: Video streaming service

In a real-time video streaming service, auto-scaling can dynamically allocate resources based on the number of viewers. During high-demand periods, additional servers can be automatically provisioned to handle the increased load.

Auto-scaling configurations in AWS can be set up to dynamically adjust the number of instances in an EC2 Auto Scaling group based on specified conditions, such as CPU utilization or network traffic.

3. **Reinforcement Learning for Resource Allocation**

Reinforcement learning techniques can be employed to optimize resource allocation in real-time AI systems, learning from past usage patterns.

Example: Cloud-based scalable AI

In a cloud-based scalable AI system, reinforcement learning algorithms can analyze historical usage data to predict peak demand periods. The system can then dynamically allocate resources to handle expected increases in workload.

Implementation of a reinforcement learning algorithm for resource allocation is complex and highly dependent on specific use cases. Libraries such as TensorFlow or PyTorch can be employed for custom implementations.

# Real-World Use Cases

1. **Healthcare Monitoring**

Real-time AI applications in healthcare use scalable systems to monitor patient data continuously. For instance, an AI system can analyze vital signs in real time, providing early warnings of potential health issues and enabling timely interventions.

2. **Autonomous Vehicles**

   Scalable AI is crucial in autonomous vehicles for real-time object recognition. As the vehicle navigates, the AI system processes streaming data from sensors to identify and respond to objects such as pedestrians and other vehicles.

3. **Smart Manufacturing**

   In smart manufacturing, scalable AI systems analyze real-time sensor data from machines to predict maintenance needs. By identifying potential issues in advance, companies can schedule maintenance activities, minimizing downtime.

Scalable AI for real-time applications is not just a technological aspiration but a necessity in today's data-driven landscape. The practices, strategies, and advanced techniques discussed in this exploration shed light on the multifaceted nature of building scalable AI systems. From the fundamental principles of parallel processing to the intricacies of reinforcement learning, each concept contributes to the overarching goal of making AI responsive, efficient, and adaptable to varying workloads.

By understanding and implementing these strategies, businesses can embark on the journey of creating AI systems that not only meet the demands of today but are also well-positioned to evolve with the ever-changing landscape of real-time applications. As we witness the transformative impact of scalable AI in healthcare, autonomous vehicles, and smart manufacturing, it becomes evident that the future of technology hinges on the ability to harness the power of AI in real time, making intelligent decisions that shape our world.

Implementing scalable AI systems in real-time environments is a multifaceted challenge that requires a combination of strategic planning, technological innovation, and a deep understanding of the specific challenges at hand. By addressing challenges such as latency management, resource allocation, data consistency, and algorithmic efficiency, organizations can pave the way for successful implementation.

The techniques discussed, ranging from microservices architecture and containerization to asynchronous processing and auto-scaling, provide practical solutions to these challenges. Embracing these techniques empowers organizations to build AI systems that not only meet the demands of real-time applications but also have the flexibility to adapt to evolving workloads. As technology advances and new challenges emerge, the collaboration between domain expertise and technological innovation will shape the future of real-time AI implementations. By employing these techniques and staying abreast of technological advancements, organizations can unlock the full potential of scalable AI systems, making informed decisions in real time and driving innovation across various industries.

You can refer to the following resources as well to know about the topic of machine learning engineering 👍:

- `https://ieeexplore.ieee.org/abstract/document/8712157`

- arXiv.org: A preprint repository that hosts research papers in various fields, including machine learning.

- Explore journals like the *Journal of Machine Learning Research, ACM Transactions on Intelligent Systems and Technology*, or *IEEE Transactions on Neural Networks and Learning Systems*. These journals often publish research papers on advanced topics in machine learning and AI infrastructure.

# CHAPTER 8

# Scalable AI for Edge Computing

AI empowers machines to mimic human intelligence, while edge computing brings computational power closer to the data source, reducing latency and enhancing efficiency. The convergence of these two trends gives rise to scalable AI for edge computing, a paradigm that aims to make intelligent applications more accessible and efficient. In this exploration, we'll unravel the key concepts, challenges, and examples that define this cutting-edge synergy.

Before getting into scalable AI for edge computing, it is critical to understand the basics of edge computing. Traditional computer models frequently feature centralized data processing, in which data is transmitted to a remote server for analysis before being given to the user. Edge computing, on the other hand, alters this paradigm by processing data closer to its source, frequently at the "edge" of the network.

Consider a smart security camera in a smart city. In a traditional setup, the camera sends video footage to a centralized server for analysis. In an edge computing scenario, the camera processes the footage, identifying potential security threats locally.

The demand for real-time, intelligent decision-making grows as AI applications become more prevalent. Edge computing is pivotal in meeting this demand, as it reduces latency, enhances reliability, and conserves bandwidth. However, the integration of AI into edge computing introduces challenges related to scalability.

## Scalability Challenges

- **Limited Resources**: Edge devices, such as IoT sensors or edge servers, often have constrained computational resources compared to powerful cloud servers.

© Abhishek Mishra 2024

A. Mishra, *Scalable AI and Design Patterns*, https://doi.org/10.1007/979-8-8688-0158-7_8

- **Heterogeneity**: Edge devices come in various shapes and sizes, each with its own set of capabilities. Scalable AI for edge computing must accommodate this heterogeneity.

- **Dynamic Environments**: Edge environments can be dynamic, with devices joining or leaving the network. Scalable AI solutions should adapt to such changes seamlessly.

While scalable AI for edge computing presents immense opportunities, several challenges and future directions merit consideration.

**Challenges**

**Security Concerns**: Edge devices are susceptible to physical attacks, making them vulnerable. Ensuring the security of AI models and data on these devices is a critical challenge.

**Interoperability**: Achieving seamless interoperability between diverse edge devices and AI models remains a challenge. Standardization efforts are crucial to address this issue.

**Future Directions**

**Edge-to-Edge Collaboration**: Exploring ways for edge devices to collaborate directly with each other, sharing insights and improving collective intelligence without relying on a central server.

**AI Model Personalization**: Customizing AI models for individual edge devices based on their usage patterns and specific requirements can further enhance performance and efficiency.

**Additional References**

Intel and NVIDIA Blog Post: "Intel, Nvidia Collaborate to Deliver Confidential AI Solutions that Strengthen AI Security, Privacy" (Oct 2022): `https://insidehpc.com/2023/07/intel-nvidia-to-collaborate-on-confidential-computing-for-ai-workloads/`

Intel Supercomputing 2023 News: "Intel Advances Scientific Research and Performance for New Wave of AI and Machine Learning" (Nov 2023): `www.intel.com/content/www/us/en/events/supercomputing.html`

NVIDIA Generative AI Solutions: `www.nvidia.com/en-us/ai-data-science/generative-ai/`

Integrating scalable AI models with edge devices opens up new possibilities across various domains, from healthcare to manufacturing and smart cities. As we navigate this evolving landscape, addressing challenges and embracing future directions will be crucial in harnessing the full potential of this powerful synergy. The journey toward scalable AI for edge computing is not just about making technology smarter; it's about making that intelligence accessible, efficient, and truly transformative for the world we live in.

# Edge Device Architectures for Scalable AI

One of the key enablers for achieving scalability is the architecture of edge devices. Edge device architectures for scalable AI play a pivotal role in distributing computational power and intelligence closer to the data source.

## Understanding Edge Device Architectures

1. **Edge Device Fundamentals**

   Edge devices are the frontline warriors in the era of distributed computing. They encompass a wide range of hardware, including IoT devices, edge servers, and smart sensors. The challenge lies in optimizing these devices to execute complex AI workloads efficiently.

2. **Scalability in AI**

   Scalability in AI refers to the ability of a system to handle an increasing amount of data and computational load. In the context of edge devices, scalability ensures that AI applications can adapt to growing demands without compromising performance.

# Best Practices for Scalable AI on Edge Devices

1. **Lightweight AI Models**

   Developing lightweight AI models is a fundamental practice for edge devices. These models strike a balance between accuracy and computational efficiency, ensuring optimal performance even on devices with limited resources.

   Example code (using TensorFlow Lite for edge devices):

   ```python
   import tensorflow as tf
   from tensorflow.lite.python.interpreter import Interpreter
   #This part imports the necessary TensorFlow modules. It brings in
   TensorFlow itself (tf) and the Interpreter class from TensorFlow
   Lite, which is used to load and run the TensorFlow Lite model.
   # Load the pre-trained lightweight model
   interpreter = Interpreter(model_path="lightweight_model.tflite")
   interpreter.allocate_tensors()

   #Here, a TensorFlow Lite Interpreter object is created by loading
   a pre-trained model. The model_path parameter specifies the path
   to the TensorFlow Lite model file (lightweight_model.tflite).
   After creating the interpreter, memory is allocated for the model
   using allocate_tensors().

   # Run inference on edge device
   input_data = ...  # Prepare input data
   interpreter.set_tensor(input_index, input_data)
   interpreter.invoke()
   output_data = interpreter.get_tensor(output_index)
   ```

   This section demonstrates the process of running inference on the edge device:

**Prepare Input Data**

You need to prepare input data (input_data) for the model. This data should match the input requirements of the loaded model.

**Set Input Tensor**

The set_tensor method is used to set the input tensor of the model. input_index is the index of the input tensor, and it is assumed to be defined elsewhere in the code.

**Invoke Inference**

invoke() is called to perform inference using the provided input data.

**Get Output Tensor**

After inference, the get_tensor method is used to retrieve the output tensor from the model. output_index is the index of the output tensor, and it is assumed to be defined elsewhere in the code.

This code snippet gives you a basic structure for running inference using a pretrained TensorFlow Lite model on an edge device. Keep in mind that you need to replace ... with the actual input data you want to feed into the model. Additionally, the values of input_index and output_index should be determined based on the model you are using.

2. **Decentralized Learning**

    Implementing decentralized learning allows edge devices to collaboratively train AI models without relying on a central server. This practice ensures adaptability and reduces dependence on a single point of failure.

    Use case: Federated learning

    Federated learning is an approach where models are trained across decentralized edge devices collaboratively. This not only improves model accuracy but also addresses privacy concerns by keeping data localized.

Reference libraries:

**PySyft**

GitHub Repository: `https://github.com/OpenMined/PySyft`

**TensorFlow Federated (TFF)**

GitHub Repository: `https://github.com/tensorflow/federated`

**PyTorch Federated Learning (PyTorch-FedLearn)**

GitHub Repository: `https://github.com/AshwinRJ/Federated-Learning-PyTorch`

These libraries provide comprehensive support for federated learning across different frameworks, making them popular choices in the federated learning community.

3. **Dynamic Resource Allocation**

Dynamic resource allocation involves adjusting computational resources based on demand and the capabilities of edge devices. This practice ensures optimal performance without overwhelming any specific device.

Advanced technique: Reinforcement learning for resource allocation

Using reinforcement learning algorithms to dynamically allocate resources based on real-time demands and device capabilities enhances the adaptability of AI systems on edge devices.

```python
# Reinforcement learning-based resource allocation
def allocate_resources(state):
    # Implement your reinforcement learning algorithm here
    action = ...
    return action

state = ...  # Define the current state
allocated_resources = allocate_resources(state)
```

# Strategies for Scalable AI on Edge Devices

1. **Edge-to-Cloud Offloading**

   Edge-to-cloud offloading involves balancing AI processing
   between edge devices and centralized cloud servers. This strategy
   optimizes resource utilization, offloading intensive tasks to the
   cloud while handling lightweight processing on the edge.

   Use case: Autonomous vehicles

   In autonomous vehicles, critical decision-making processes can
   be offloaded to the cloud, while edge devices handle real-time
   tasks like obstacle detection.

2. **Containerization**

   Containerization enables the packaging of AI models and their
   dependencies into lightweight, portable containers. This strategy
   streamlines deployment across diverse edge devices with different
   architectures.

   Advanced technique: Kubernetes for edge device orchestration

   Using Kubernetes to orchestrate containers on edge devices
   facilitates efficient scaling and management of AI workloads.

```yaml
# Kubernetes deployment configuration for edge devices
apiVersion: apps/v1
kind: Deployment
metadata:
  name: edge-ai-deployment
spec:
  replicas: 3
  selector:
    matchLabels:
      app: edge-ai
  template:
    metadata:
```

```
          labels:
            app: edge-ai
      spec:
        containers:
        - name: ai-container
          image: your-edge-ai-image:latest
```

3. **Edge Device Collaboration**

   Enabling collaboration between edge devices enhances the
   collective intelligence of the system. This strategy involves devices
   sharing insights and knowledge, fostering a collaborative AI
   ecosystem.

   Use case: Smart grids

In a smart grid, edge devices collaborate to optimize energy distribution based on
real-time data, ensuring efficient resource utilization.

# Advanced Techniques for Edge Device Architectures

1. **Neuromorphic Computing**

   Neuromorphic computing mimics the structure and functionality
   of the human brain. Implementing neuromorphic architectures
   on edge devices can significantly enhance AI processing
   efficiency.

   Example: IBM TrueNorth chip

   The TrueNorth chip from IBM is an example of a neuromorphic
   computing architecture that excels in pattern recognition tasks,
   making it suitable for edge devices in AI applications.

2. **Quantum Computing at the Edge**

   Quantum computing introduces the potential for exponential
   speedup in certain AI computations. Integrating quantum
   computing capabilities at the edge can revolutionize the
   processing power of AI systems.

Future direction: Quantum edge devices

Research is ongoing to develop quantum processors suitable for edge devices, bringing the benefits of quantum computing to the forefront of AI on the edge.

# Real-World Examples of Scalable AI on Edge Devices

1. **Healthcare: Edge AI for Medical Imaging**

   Scenario: Edge devices equipped with AI algorithms analyze medical imaging data in real time. Lightweight models running on these devices enable quick and accurate diagnosis without relying on centralized servers.

2. **Retail: Edge AI for Customer Analytics**

   Scenario: Edge devices in retail stores process customer behavior data locally, providing real-time analytics. This enhances customer experiences without the need for continuous cloud connectivity.

3. **Agriculture: Precision Farming with Edge AI**

   Scenario: Edge devices installed on agricultural machinery analyze soil conditions and crop health in real time. This enables precision farming practices, optimizing resource usage without constant reliance on the cloud.

# Future Directions and Challenges in Edge Device Architectures

**Challenges**

1. **Energy Efficiency**: Ensuring that edge devices operate efficiently in terms of power consumption remains a significant challenge.

2. **Security**: Edge devices are susceptible to physical attacks, emphasizing the need for robust security measures to protect AI models and data.

In the ever-evolving landscape of AI and edge computing, the architecture of edge devices stands as a linchpin for scalability and efficiency. Best practices, strategies, and advanced techniques discussed in this exploration provide a road map for designing scalable AI systems on edge devices. As we navigate the challenges and embrace future directions, the synergy between scalable AI and edge device architectures holds the promise of transforming industries and making intelligent applications more accessible than ever before. The journey toward scalable AI on edge devices is not just a technological evolution; it's a revolution shaping the future of AI at the edge.

# Edge AI Model Optimization

Edge AI Model Optimization is a critical facet of harnessing the full potential of artificial intelligence at the edge. As devices become more intelligent, the need for efficient, lightweight models that can run seamlessly on resource-constrained edge devices becomes paramount.

At its core, Edge AI Model Optimization is about crafting machine learning models that strike a balance between accuracy and computational efficiency, ensuring they can operate effectively on devices with limited resources. This process involves various strategies aimed at reducing the model's size, complexity, and inference time without compromising its predictive capabilities.

# Practices for Edge AI Model Optimization

1.  **Quantization**

    Quantization involves reducing the precision of the model's parameters, typically from 32-bit floating-point numbers to 8-bit integers. This significantly decreases the model size and speeds up inference, making it ideal for edge devices.

    Example code:

    ```python
    import tensorflow as tf
    converter = tf.lite.TFLiteConverter.from_saved_model(saved_
    model_dir)
    ```

```
converter.optimizations = [tf.lite.Optimize.DEFAULT]
tflite_quant_model = converter.convert()
```

The provided Python code utilizes TensorFlow to convert a
pretrained model, saved in the TensorFlow SavedModel format,
into a quantized TensorFlow Lite model. The process involves
creating a "TFLiteConverter" object, specifying the SavedModel
directory, and setting optimization options, particularly
employing default optimizations like quantization to reduce
model size. The final step invokes the "convert()" method on
the converter, generating the quantized TensorFlow Lite model
("tflite_quant_model"). This type of conversion is valuable for
deploying machine learning models on edge devices where
resource efficiency is crucial, as the quantized model consumes
less memory and potentially speeds up inference.

2. **Pruning**

   Pruning involves removing unnecessary connections (weights)
   from the model, leading to a sparser, more efficient structure. This
   reduces the model size and accelerates inference.

   Example code:

   ```python
   from tensorflow_model_optimization.sparsity import keras as
   sparsity
   pruned_model = sparsity.prune_low_magnitude(original_model)
   pruned_model.compile(optimizer='adam', loss='sparse_
   categorical_crossentropy', metrics=['accuracy'])
   pruned_model.fit(x_train, y_train, epochs=5)
   ```

   The provided Python code demonstrates model pruning using the
   TensorFlow Model Optimization library. It imports the "prune_
   low_magnitude" function from "tensorflow_model_optimization.
   sparsity.keras" and applies it to the "original_model", creating
   a pruned model ("pruned_model"). The pruned model is then

```
```

compiled with the specified optimizer, loss function, and metrics using the "compile" method. Finally, the pruned model is trained on the training data ("x_train" and "y_train") for a specified number of epochs (in this case, 5) using the "fit" method. Model pruning is a technique that involves removing certain connections or weights in a neural network, resulting in a sparser and potentially more efficient model.

3. **Knowledge Distillation**

   Knowledge distillation involves training a smaller model (student) to mimic the behavior of a larger, more complex model (teacher). This helps in transferring the knowledge of the larger model to a more compact one.

   Example code:

```python
from tensorflow import keras
teacher_model = keras.models.load_model('teacher_model.h5')
student_model = create_student_model()
distiller = Distiller(student=student_model,
teacher=teacher_model)
distiller.compile(
    optimizer=keras.optimizers.Adam(learning_rate=1e-3),
    metrics=[keras.metrics.CategoricalAccuracy()],
    student_loss_fn=keras.losses.CategoricalCrossentropy(),
    distillation_loss_fn=keras.losses.KLDivergence(),
    alpha=0.1,
    temperature=10,
)
```

   The provided Python code exemplifies model distillation using TensorFlow and Keras. It loads a preexisting teacher model ("teacher_model") from the "teacher_model.h5" file and creates a student model ("student_model") using a function called "create_student_model". A "distiller" is then instantiated with the student and teacher models. The "compile" method is used to configure the distiller with an Adam optimizer, categorical accuracy metric, student loss function (categorical cross-entropy), distillation loss function (Kullback-Leibler divergence), and additional parameters such as alpha and temperature. Model distillation is a technique where a smaller student model is trained to replicate the behavior of a larger teacher model, aiming to transfer the knowledge encoded in the teacher to the student for more efficient deployment.

# Strategies for Scalable AI Systems

Optimizing AI models for edge devices is not a one-time endeavor; it requires a strategic approach to ensure scalability and adaptability. Let's explore key strategies for building scalable AI systems at the edge.

1. **Model Architecture Design**

   Choosing the right model architecture is foundational. Smaller architectures with fewer parameters generally perform better on edge devices. Consider trade-offs between complexity and accuracy.

   Example code:

   ```python
   from tensorflow.keras.models import Sequential
   from tensorflow.keras.layers import Dense, Conv2D,
   MaxPooling2D, Flatten

   model = Sequential([
       Conv2D(32, (3, 3), activation='relu', input_shape=(224,
       224, 3)),
       MaxPooling2D((2, 2)),
       Flatten(),
       Dense(128, activation='relu'),
       Dense(10, activation='softmax')
   ])
   ```

2. **Transfer Learning**

Leverage pretrained models and fine-tune them for specific edge tasks. This reduces the need for extensive training on edge devices.

Example code:

```python
from tensorflow.keras.applications import MobileNetV2
from tensorflow.keras.models import Sequential
from tensorflow.keras.layers import Dense,
GlobalAveragePooling2D

base_model = MobileNetV2(weights='imagenet', include_
top=False)
model = Sequential([
    base_model,
    GlobalAveragePooling2D(),
    Dense(10, activation='softmax')
])
```

3. **Hardware Acceleration**

Leverage hardware accelerators, such as GPUs or TPUs, to boost the inference speed of AI models on edge devices.

Example code (TensorFlow with GPU):

```python
import tensorflow as tf
physical_devices = tf.config.list_physical_devices('GPU')
if physical_devices:
    tf.config.experimental.set_memory_growth(physical_
    devices[0], True)
```

As the field of edge AI evolves, advanced techniques emerge to address the ever-growing demand for intelligent applications on edge devices:

1. **Neural Architecture Search (NAS)**

   NAS involves automating the design of neural network architectures and searching for the optimal structure that meets specific performance criteria.

   Example code (using AutoKeras):

   ```python
   !pip install autokeras
   import autokeras as ak
   clf = ak.ImageClassifier(overwrite=True, max_trials=1)
   self.fit(x_train, y_train, epochs=10)
   ```

2. **Edge-to-Cloud Collaboration**

   Distributing tasks between edge devices and cloud servers allows complex computations to be offloaded to the cloud, reducing the load on edge devices.

   Example code (edge device):

   ```python
   # Inference code running on edge device
   result = edge_model.predict(input_data)
   ```

   Example code (cloud server):

   ```python
   # Additional processing in the cloud
   result_analysis = cloud_model_analyze(result)
   ```

# Real-World Use Cases

Let's explore real-world use cases where Edge AI Model Optimization plays a pivotal role:

1. **Smart Cameras for Surveillance**

   Deploying smart cameras with optimized AI models for real-time object detection. The models efficiently process video streams on the edge, minimizing latency in security surveillance systems.

2. **Voice Assistants on IoT Devices**

   Implementing optimized natural language processing models on IoT devices to enable voice assistants. The models understand and respond to user commands locally, enhancing user experience and privacy.

3. **Autonomous Vehicles**

   Integrating optimized machine learning models for object detection and decision-making in autonomous vehicles. The models run on edge devices within the vehicle, ensuring real-time responses to the surrounding environment.

Edge AI Model Optimization is a dynamic field that bridges the gap between the power of artificial intelligence and the constraints of edge devices. From quantization to advanced techniques like neural architecture search, the journey to scalable AI systems at the edge involves a thoughtful combination of practices and strategies. As we navigate this landscape, real-world examples and code snippets serve as beacons, guiding the way toward efficient, accessible, and transformative AI applications on the edge. The future of intelligent edge computing is not just about optimization; it's about unlocking the full potential of AI to make our devices smarter, faster, and more adaptive to the world around us.

# Edge-to-Cloud Integration for Scalable AI

In the fast-paced realm of technology, the integration of edge computing and cloud computing has emerged as a transformative force, particularly in the context of artificial intelligence (AI). This convergence gives rise to edge-to-cloud integration for scalable AI, a paradigm that seeks to leverage the strengths of both edge and cloud environments to create intelligent systems that are not only efficient but also scalable.

Edge computing involves processing data closer to the source, reducing latency, and enhancing real-time decision-making. Edge devices, such as sensors and edge servers, play a crucial role in this paradigm by performing computations locally.

Cloud computing, on the other hand, relies on centralized servers to process and store data. It offers vast computational resources and is well suited for complex tasks that demand substantial processing power.

Edge-to-cloud integration aims to harmonize the strengths of both edge and cloud computing. In this synergy, edge devices handle time-sensitive tasks locally, while the cloud manages resource-intensive computations and storage. This integration is especially relevant for AI applications that require both real-time responsiveness and the processing power of the cloud.

# Practices for Scalable AI in Edge-to-Cloud Integration

1. **Edge-Friendly Model Deployment**

   Deploying AI models at the edge requires careful consideration of resource constraints. Edge devices often have limited computational power and memory. Therefore, designing models that are optimized for edge deployment is crucial.

   Example:

   ```python
   # TensorFlow Lite for Edge Deployment
   import tensorflow as tf

   # Load the model
   model = tf.keras.models.load_model('edge_friendly_model.h5')

   # Convert the model to TensorFlow Lite format
   converter = tf.lite.TFLiteConverter.from_keras_model(model)
   tflite_model = converter.convert()
   ```

```python
# Save the TensorFlow Lite model
with open('edge_friendly_model.tflite', 'wb') as f:
    f.write(tflite_model)
```

2. **Decentralized Learning and Federated Learning**

In edge-to-cloud integration, training models in a decentralized manner is beneficial. Federated learning enables edge devices to collaboratively train models without sending raw data to the cloud, preserving privacy.

Example:

```python
# PySyft for Federated Learning
import syft as sy
import torch

# Hook PyTorch to PySyft
hook = sy.TorchHook(torch)

# Create virtual workers representing edge devices
alice = sy.VirtualWorker(hook, id="alice")
bob = sy.VirtualWorker(hook, id="bob")

# Define the model and optimizer
model = torch.nn.Linear(2, 1)
optimizer = torch.optim.SGD(model.parameters(), lr=0.01)

# Perform federated learning
for epoch in range(10):
    # Train on Alice's data
    model = model.send(alice)
    optimizer.zero_grad()
    output = model(torch.tensor([[1.0, 1.0]]))
    loss = ((output - torch.tensor([[2.0]]))**2).sum()
    loss.backward()
```

```python
    optimizer.step()
    model = model.get()

    # Train on Bob's data
    model = model.send(bob)
    optimizer.zero_grad()
    output = model(torch.tensor([[0.0, 0.0]]))
    loss = ((output - torch.tensor([[0.0]]))**2).sum()
    loss.backward()
    optimizer.step()
    model = model.get()
```

3. **Dynamic Resource Allocation**

Efficient resource allocation is crucial in edge-to-cloud integration. Dynamic allocation ensures optimal utilization of resources based on the demand and capabilities of edge devices.

Example:

```python
# Dynamic Resource Allocation in Python
class EdgeResourceManager:
    def __init__(self, edge_devices):
        self.edge_devices = edge_devices
        self.available_resources = {device: 100 for device in
        edge_devices}

    def allocate_resources(self, device, resources_needed):
        if self.available_resources[device] >= resources_needed:
            self.available_resources[device] -= resources_needed
            print(f"Allocated {resources_needed} resources to
            {device}")
        else:
            print(f"Not enough resources on {device}")
```

```python
# Example usage
edge_devices = ["EdgeDevice1", "EdgeDevice2", "EdgeDevice3"]
resource_manager = EdgeResourceManager(edge_devices)
resource_manager.allocate_resources("EdgeDevice1", 30)
```

# Strategies for Effective Edge-to-Cloud Integration

1. **Data Filtering and Preprocessing at Edge**

   To reduce the burden on the cloud and minimize data transfer, perform data filtering and preprocessing at the edge. Edge devices can filter out irrelevant data and send only essential information to the cloud.

   Example:

   ```python
   # Edge Data Filtering and Preprocessing
   def edge_data_processing(sensor_data):
       # Perform filtering and preprocessing
       processed_data = filter_and_preprocess(sensor_data)
       return processed_data

   # Example usage
   sensor_data = collect_sensor_data()
   processed_data = edge_data_processing(sensor_data)
   cloud_result = send_to_cloud_for_processing(processed_data)
   ```

   The provided Python code illustrates an example of edge data processing. The function "edge_data_processing" takes "sensor_data" as input, performs filtering and preprocessing using a hypothetical function "filter_and_preprocess", and returns the processed data. This function represents a common scenario in edge computing where raw sensor data is initially processed locally on the edge device before being sent to the cloud for further analysis. In this example, "collect_sensor_data" is a placeholder for a function that gathers sensor data. The processed data is then sent to the cloud for additional processing using the function "send_to_cloud_for_processing". This approach helps reduce the amount of raw data transmitted to the cloud, improving efficiency and reducing latency in edge computing applications.

2. **Asynchronous Communication Between Edge and Cloud**

Utilize asynchronous communication to allow edge devices to operate independently while communicating with the cloud in a non-blocking manner. This enhances the responsiveness of the system.

Example:

```python
# Asynchronous Communication in Python
import asyncio

async def edge_task():
    while True:
        # Perform edge computations
        result = perform_edge_computation()

        # Send result to cloud asynchronously
        asyncio.ensure_future(send_to_cloud(result))

        # Continue with edge computations
        continue_processing()

async def send_to_cloud(result):
    # Simulate asynchronous communication with the cloud
    await asyncio.sleep(2)
    print(f"Result sent to cloud: {result}")

# Run the edge task
asyncio.run(edge_task())
```

The provided Python code demonstrates an example of asynchronous communication in Python using the "asyncio" library. The "edge_task" function represents an asynchronous task running on an edge device. Within this task, continuous edge computations are performed, and the results are sent to the cloud asynchronously using the "send_to_cloud" function. The "send_to_cloud" function simulates asynchronous communication by introducing a sleep of two seconds (representing network latency or other asynchronous operations). The "asyncio.ensure_future" method is used to concurrently execute the "send_to_cloud" function without blocking the main edge computation loop. This asynchronous approach allows the edge device to perform computations and communicate with the cloud concurrently, enhancing the efficiency of edge computing applications. Finally, the "asyncio.run(edge_task())" statement initiates the execution of the edge task.

3. **Hybrid Model Deployment**

Deploying a hybrid model that combines elements of edge and cloud processing offers flexibility. The model can dynamically offload tasks to the cloud based on resource availability and requirements.

Example:

```python
# Hybrid Model Deployment in Python
class HybridModel:
    def __init__(self, edge_model, cloud_model):
        self.edge_model = edge_model
        self.cloud_model = cloud_model

    def predict(self, data):
        if is_edge_available():
            return self.edge_model.predict(data)
        else:
            return self.cloud_model.predict(data)
```

```
# Example usage
edge_model = load_edge_model()
cloud_model = load_cloud_model()
hybrid_model = HybridModel(edge_model, cloud_model)
result = hybrid_model.predict(input_data)
```

The provided Python code illustrates an example of hybrid model deployment, allowing dynamic selection between an edge model and a cloud model based on the availability of edge resources. The "HybridModel" class is defined with an initialization method that takes an edge model and a cloud model as parameters. The "predict" method of this class checks whether the edge resources are available using the "is_edge_available" function. If edge resources are available, it utilizes the edge model for prediction; otherwise, it falls back to the cloud model.

In the example usage, edge and cloud models are loaded, and an instance of the "HybridModel" class is created with these models. The "predict" method is then called with input data, and the result is obtained, demonstrating the flexibility of hybrid model deployment based on the availability of edge resources. This approach is beneficial for optimizing model execution by leveraging local edge resources when possible and resorting to cloud resources when needed.

# Advanced Techniques in Edge-to-Cloud Integration

1. **Edge Caching for Reduced Latency**

   Implement edge caching to store frequently used data or model parameters at the edge. This reduces the need to fetch data from the cloud repeatedly, minimizing latency.

   Example:

```python
# Edge Caching in Python
class EdgeCache:
    def __init__(self):
        self.cache = {}
```

```python
    def get_data(self, key):
        if key in
  self.cache:
            print(f"Retrieved {key} from edge cache")
            return self.cache[key]
        else:
            print(f"{key} not found in edge cache")
            return None

    def set_data(self, key, data):
        print(f"Stored {key} in edge cache")

        self.cache[key] = data

# Example usage
edge_cache = EdgeCache()
data = edge_cache.get_data("sensor_data")

if data is None:
    # Fetch data from the cloud
    data = fetch_data_from_cloud("sensor_data")
    edge_cache.set_data("sensor_data", data)
```

The provided Python code demonstrates an example of edge caching using the "EdgeCache" class. This class has methods to get data ("get_data") and set data ("set_data"). The "get_data" method checks if the requested data is present in the edge cache. If found, it retrieves and prints the data; otherwise, it prints that the data is not found. The "set_data" method stores the provided data in the edge cache and prints a corresponding message.

In the example usage, an instance of the "EdgeCache" class ("edge_cache") is created. The "get_data" method is then called to retrieve "sensor_data" from the edge cache. If the data is not present (returns "None"), the code fetches the data from the cloud using the hypothetical function "fetch_data_from_cloud" and then stores it in the edge cache using the "set_data" method.

This illustrates a simple implementation of edge caching, a technique that can enhance the efficiency of edge devices by locally storing and retrieving frequently used data, reducing the need for repeated retrieval from the cloud.

2. **Edge Intelligence for Real-Time Inference**

Empower edge devices with intelligence to perform real-time inference. This reduces the reliance on the cloud for inference tasks, enhancing responsiveness.

Example:

```python
# Edge Intelligence for Real-time Inference
class EdgeInferenceModel:
    def __init__(self, edge_model):
        self.edge_model = edge_model

    def perform_inference(self, data):
        # Perform real-time inference at the edge
        result = self.edge_model.predict(data)
        return result

# Example usage
edge_model = load_edge_inference_model()
edge_inference_model = EdgeInferenceModel(edge_model)
real_time_result = edge_inference_model.perform_inference(real_time_data)
```

The provided Python code demonstrates the implementation of edge intelligence for real-time inference using the "EdgeInferenceModel" class. This class is initialized with an edge model, and it has a method named "perform_inference" for conducting real-time inference at the edge.

In the example usage, an edge model is loaded, and an instance of the "EdgeInferenceModel" class ("edge_inference_model") is created with this edge model. The "perform_inference" method is

143

then called with real-time data ("real_time_data"), and the result of the inference is stored in the "real_time_result" variable.

This example showcases how edge intelligence can be utilized for making real-time inferences at the edge, demonstrating the capability of edge devices to process data locally without relying on cloud resources.

3. **Adaptive Learning Rates for Edge Training**

Implement adaptive learning rates during edge training to ensure that models converge efficiently. This dynamic adjustment of learning rates enhances the training process on resource-constrained edge devices.

Example:

```python
# Adaptive Learning Rates for Edge Training
class AdaptiveLearningRateOptimizer:
    def __init__(self, base_learning_rate):
        self.base_learning_rate = base_learning_rate
        self.current_learning_rate = base_learning_rate

    def adjust_learning_rate(self, performance_metric):
        # Adjust learning rate based on performance metric
        if performance_metric < threshold:
            self.current_learning_rate *= 0.9
        else:
            self.current_learning_rate *= 1.1

        print(f"Adjusted learning rate to {self.current_
        learning_rate}")

# Example usage
base_learning_rate = 0.01
optimizer = AdaptiveLearningRateOptimizer(base_learning_rate)
train_model(optimizer)
```

The provided Python code illustrates the implementation of adaptive learning rates for edge training using the "AdaptiveLearningRateOptimizer" class. This optimizer is initialized with a base learning rate, and it has a method named "adjust_learning_rate" for dynamically adjusting the learning rate based on a performance metric.

In the example usage, a base learning rate of "0.01" is set, and an instance of the "AdaptiveLearningRateOptimizer" class ("optimizer") is created with this base learning rate. The "train_model" function is then called with this optimizer, indicating that the model training process will adaptively adjust the learning rate based on the specified performance metric during training.

This example showcases how adaptive learning rates can be employed to enhance the training process for edge models, allowing the learning rate to be dynamically modified based on the model's performance.

**Real-World Use Cases**

1. **Smart Agriculture: Crop Monitoring**

   In a smart agriculture system, edge devices equipped with sensors monitor crop conditions. Edge AI models analyze the sensor data locally to identify issues such as pest infestations or nutrient deficiencies. Critical insights are sent to the cloud for comprehensive analysis, enabling farmers to make informed decisions.

2. **Retail: In-Store Customer Analytics**

   In a retail setting, edge devices with cameras capture customer behavior. Edge AI processes the video feed locally to extract customer analytics, such as foot traffic patterns and popular product zones. Aggregated data is then sent to the cloud for deeper analysis, helping retailers optimize store layouts and promotions.

3. **Healthcare: Wearable Devices for Patient Monitoring**

   Wearable devices equipped with AI capabilities continuously monitor patients' health parameters. Edge AI processes real-time data locally to detect anomalies and trigger immediate alerts if necessary. Aggregated data, including historical trends, is periodically sent to the cloud for long-term analysis and personalized healthcare recommendations.

145

In the dynamic landscape of AI, the integration of edge computing and cloud computing opens avenues for scalable and efficient systems. Edge-to-cloud integration for scalable AI involves a thoughtful combination of practices, strategies, and advanced techniques. Deploying edge-friendly models, embracing decentralized learning, and implementing dynamic resource allocation are foundational practices. Strategies such as asynchronous communication, hybrid model deployment, and data filtering at the edge enhance system responsiveness and efficiency.

Advanced techniques like edge caching, edge intelligence, and adaptive learning rates further elevate the capabilities of edge-to-cloud integration. Real-world use cases in smart agriculture, retail, and healthcare illustrate the practical application of these concepts, showcasing the transformative impact of scalable AI systems.

As we navigate the evolving landscape of technology, the integration of edge and cloud continues to be a driving force, offering not just scalability but also the promise of intelligent systems that seamlessly blend the power of local processing with the vast resources of the cloud.

Scalable AI catalyzes unlocking the full potential of edge computing, enabling intelligent applications that operate closer to the data source. This integration not only minimizes latency but also optimizes resource utilization, making AI more accessible to devices with limited computational capabilities.

The unique characteristics of edge devices, such as constrained resources and diverse form factors, necessitate specialized approaches. Scalable AI, in this context, involves the deployment of edge-friendly models, the implementation of decentralized learning, and dynamic resource allocation. These practices ensure that AI applications seamlessly adapt to the constraints of edge environments, fostering efficiency and responsiveness.

As we navigate this intersection of scalable AI and edge computing, it is clear that the combination of these technologies opens doors to innovative solutions across various domains. Whether in healthcare, manufacturing, or smart cities, the application of scalable AI in edge computing environments is paving the way for intelligent systems that not only meet the specific needs of edge devices but also contribute to a more interconnected and intelligent world.

# CHAPTER 9

# Scalable AI Governance and Ethics

Artificial intelligence (AI) has become an integral part of our lives, influencing how we work, communicate, and make decisions. As AI technologies advance, the need for robust governance and ethical frameworks becomes increasingly crucial. AI governance refers to the set of policies, procedures, and regulations designed to guide the development, deployment, and use of AI systems. It serves as a compass, ensuring that AI aligns with human values, legal standards, and societal expectations.

Readers interested in exploring implementations, use cases, and projects related to Trusted AI can refer to the GitHub repository: `https://github.com/Trusted-AI`.

This repository likely contains valuable resources, code, and documentation related to Trusted AI, offering a deeper understanding of the implementations, use cases, and projects within the Trusted AI domain. For an in-depth exploration, readers are encouraged to visit the provided GitHub repository.

## The Importance of AI Governance

### Accountability

Example: Imagine an AI system used in a healthcare setting. If the AI makes a wrong diagnosis, accountability measures established through governance frameworks help identify responsibility, whether it's the developers, users, or the AI itself.

### Transparency

Example: An AI algorithm determines whether a loan application is approved or denied. Transparent AI governance ensures that the decision-making process is understandable and can be explained to the loan applicant.

147

A. Mishra, *Scalable AI and Design Patterns*, https://doi.org/10.1007/979-8-8688-0158-7_9

**Fairness**

Example: In hiring processes where AI is involved, governance ensures that the AI doesn't discriminate based on gender, race, or other protected characteristics, promoting fairness in employment opportunities.

# Principles of Scalable AI Governance

**Human-Centric Design**

Example: When developing AI applications for elderly care, a human-centric approach involves designing interfaces and functionalities that cater to the unique needs and preferences of older individuals.

**Continuous Monitoring and Adaptation**

Example: An AI system used in financial transactions is subject to changing regulations. A scalable governance model involves continuous monitoring and adaptation to ensure compliance with evolving legal standards.

**Interdisciplinary Collaboration**

Example: The development of an AI system for climate modeling requires collaboration between climate scientists, AI experts, and ethicists. Scalable governance encourages interdisciplinary teamwork to address diverse perspectives and challenges.

# Technical Implementation

**Explainability and Interpretability**

Example: In the criminal justice system, an AI tool predicting recidivism must provide explanations for its decisions. Scalable governance mandates the incorporation of explainability features, allowing users to understand the reasoning behind AI outputs.

**Data Governance**

Example: A healthcare AI relies on patient data. Scalable governance ensures that data collection, storage, and usage adhere to strict privacy and security standards, protecting sensitive information from unauthorized access.

**Robustness and Security**

Example: Autonomous drones used in agriculture need to withstand environmental challenges. Scalable governance requires AI developers to prioritize robustness, ensuring the technology can operate effectively in various conditions while safeguarding against malicious attacks.

Scalable AI governance and ethics represent the compass guiding the responsible development and deployment of AI technologies. By understanding the foundational principles, technical implementations, challenges, and real-world applications, we can navigate the complexities of this rapidly evolving landscape. As we envision the future, the collaborative efforts of diverse stakeholders will be crucial in shaping a world where AI benefits humanity ethically and sustainably.

# Bias Mitigation and Fairness in Scalable AI

In the dynamic landscape of artificial intelligence (AI), one of the critical challenges we face is mitigating bias and ensuring fairness in scalable AI systems. As AI applications permeate various aspects of our lives, from hiring decisions to medical diagnoses, it becomes imperative to develop practices and strategies that not only identify and rectify biases but also ensure these approaches are scalable.

In the dynamic landscape of artificial intelligence (AI), one of the critical challenges we face is mitigating bias and ensuring fairness in scalable AI systems. As AI applications permeate various aspects of our lives, from hiring decisions to medical diagnoses, it becomes imperative to develop practices and strategies that not only identify and rectify biases but also ensure these approaches are scalable.

## Understanding Bias in AI

Bias in AI refers to the presence of systematic and unfair inaccuracies in the decision-making processes of AI algorithms. These biases can emerge from the data used to train the AI models, reflecting historical inequalities or prejudices present in the data.

### Types of Bias with Examples

1. **Selection Bias**

   In a hiring AI system trained on historical data, if certain demographics were underrepresented, the model may perpetuate this bias by favoring those demographics.

2. **Sampling Bias**

   An AI model predicting customer preferences in a specific market might be biased if the training data only includes a particular segment of the population.

149

3.  **Confirmation Bias**

An AI-powered news recommendation system might inadvertently reinforce users' existing beliefs by consistently suggesting content that aligns with their viewpoints.

# The Importance of Fairness in Scalable AI

1.  **Ethical Considerations**

If an AI-driven loan approval system consistently denies loans to a particular ethnic group, it raises ethical concerns regarding fairness and equal opportunity.

2.  **Legal Implications**

Discrimination in hiring decisions made by AI systems may lead to legal repercussions, necessitating a commitment to fairness to comply with anti-discrimination laws.

3.  **User Trust and Adoption**

If users perceive an AI system as biased, they are less likely to trust its recommendations, limiting the system's effectiveness and adoption.

# Practices for Bias Mitigation in Scalable AI

1.  **Diverse and Representative Training Data**

In facial recognition systems, ensuring diverse representation in the training dataset helps mitigate biases related to race, gender, and other demographic factors.

2.  **Data Augmentation**

In natural language processing models, augmenting the training data with synonymous phrases helps expose the model to a broader range of linguistic expressions, reducing language-based biases.

3. **Fair Feature Engineering**

   In credit scoring models, instead of using sensitive features like race or gender, incorporate alternative features that capture creditworthiness without introducing bias.

4. **Regularized Models**

   Adding penalty terms to the model training process for coefficients associated with sensitive attributes discourages the model from relying on those attributes.

5. **Reweighting Instances**

   Giving different weights to instances in the training data based on their potential bias, adjusting the learning process to prioritize fair predictions.

6. **Calibration**

   In predictive policing, calibrating the model's output to ensure that predicted crime rates align with actual observed rates across different demographic groups.

# Advanced Techniques for Scalable Fairness

**Adversarial Training**

1. Definition:

   Adversarial training involves introducing adversarial examples into the training data to teach the model to be robust against attempts to introduce biases.

2. Example:

   In a healthcare AI predicting disease prevalence, synthetic data challenges the model's understanding of disease prevalence in different demographics.

**Counterfactual Fairness**

1. Definition:

   – Counterfactual fairness aims to ensure that individuals would be treated the same by an AI model regardless of their membership in a protected group, even when considering counterfactual scenarios.

2. Example:

   – In a loan approval system, ensuring that if an applicant from one demographic group were in the position of another, the decision would remain consistent.

**Explainable AI (XAI)**

1. Definition:

   – Explainable AI focuses on making AI models more interpretable, enabling stakeholders to understand how decisions are made and identify potential biases.

2. Example:

   – In a criminal justice AI, providing explanations for why a particular individual is deemed at high risk of reoffending allows for scrutiny and accountability.

# Real-World Use Cases

**Fairness in Hiring**

1. Challenge:

   – AI-driven hiring platforms can unintentionally favor certain demographics, perpetuating historical biases in employment.

2. Solution:

   – Implementing fairness-aware algorithms that ensure equal opportunity for all applicants, regardless of demographic factors.

**Healthcare Diagnoses**

1.  Challenge:

    –   Biases in healthcare AI can lead to disparities in diagnoses and treatment recommendations across different patient groups.

2.  Solution:

    –   Deploying models that consider a diverse range of patient populations during training, ensuring equitable healthcare outcomes.

**Criminal Justice System**

1.  Challenge:

    –   Predictive policing AI may inadvertently reinforce biases present in historical crime data.

2.  Solution:

    –   Applying fairness-enhancing techniques to prevent the model from disproportionately targeting specific communities.

# Code Implementation Example

Python Code for Bias Mitigation

```python
```python
Example of re-weighting instances to mitigate bias
from sklearn.utils.class_weight import compute_sample_weight
from sklearn.model_selection import train_test_split
from sklearn.linear_model import LogisticRegression

Load your dataset
X, y, sample_weights = load_data()

Split the data
X_train, X_test, y_train, y_test, weights_train, weights_test = train_test_
split(X, y, sample_weights, test_size=0.2)

Initialize the model
model = LogisticRegression()
```
```

```
Fit the model with re-weighted instances
model.fit(X_train, y_train, sample_weight=weights_train)

 Evaluate the model
accuracy = model.score(X_test, y_test, sample_weight=weights_test)
```

This code snippet demonstrates how to reweight instances in a logistic regression model to mitigate bias based on sample weights.

# Challenges and Future Directions

1. **Intersectionality**

   – Adapting AI fairness techniques to consider the intersectionality of multiple protected attributes remains a challenge.

2. **Dynamic Bias**

   – Addressing biases that emerge dynamically as societal norms and perceptions change over time.

**Future Directions**

1. **Ethical AI Education**

   – Integrating ethical AI education into the training of AI professionals to foster a proactive approach to fairness.

2. **Community Involvement**

   – Engaging communities in the development and assessment of AI systems to ensure diverse perspectives are considered.

In the realm of scalable AI, the journey toward bias mitigation and fairness is a continuous exploration. Through effective data preprocessing, model development practices, and advanced techniques like adversarial training and counterfactual fairness, we can build AI systems that not only make accurate predictions but do so ethically and fairly. Real-world use cases highlight the impact of these strategies in various domains, from hiring to healthcare. As we navigate the challenges and envision the future, it is our collective responsibility to nurture ethical intelligence in AI, ensuring that these transformative technologies benefit society equitably.

# Interpretability in Scalable AI Models: Navigating the Complexities

Artificial intelligence (AI) models have evolved significantly, becoming more powerful and complex. As these models scale in size and capability, the need for interpretability becomes paramount. Interpretability refers to the ability to understand and explain how AI models make decisions.

Interpretability in the context of AI models involves making the decision-making process of these models understandable to humans. It addresses the "black box" nature of complex algorithms, enabling users to trust, validate, and troubleshoot AI outputs.

**Why Is Interpretability Important in Scalable AI Models?**

1. **Trust and Accountability**

   – Example: Imagine a large financial institution using an AI model to assess loan applications. If the model denies a loan, stakeholders need to understand the factors influencing the decision. Interpretability builds trust by providing transparent insights into the decision-making process.

2. **Ethical Considerations**

   – Example: In healthcare, where AI assists in diagnostics, interpretability ensures that doctors and patients can comprehend the reasoning behind a diagnosis. This transparency is essential for ethical decision-making and patient trust.

3. **Regulatory Compliance**

   – Example: With the General Data Protection Regulation (GDPR) and similar regulations in place, businesses using AI must ensure compliance. Interpretability helps in explaining to regulatory bodies how AI models process and utilize personal data.

# Practices for Interpretability in Scalable AI Models

## Foundational Practices

1. **Feature Importance Analysis**

   – Explanation: Identify which features or variables have the most significant impact on model predictions.

   – Example: In a retail setting, if an AI model predicts product sales, feature importance analysis reveals which factors, such as price or promotions, influence the predictions the most.

2. **Model-Agnostic Techniques**

   – Explanation: Techniques that are not tied to a specific algorithm, making them applicable to various models.

   – Example: LIME (Local Interpretable Model-Agnostic Explanations) generates locally faithful interpretations for any black-box model, aiding in understanding specific predictions.

3. **Sensitivity Analysis**

   – Explanation: Assess the impact of small changes in input variables on model outputs.

   – Example: In climate modeling, sensitivity analysis helps understand how slight alterations in temperature or precipitation data influence long-term predictions.

## Strategies for Scalability

1. **Data Subset Analysis**

   – Explanation: Analyzing a representative subset of the data to provide insights into model behavior without processing the entire dataset.

   – Example: In financial fraud detection, analyzing a subset of recent transactions helps identify patterns and interpret the model's decision-making without the need to process all historical data.

2. **Ensemble Models**

   – Explanation: Combining predictions from multiple models to enhance accuracy and interpretability.

   – Example: In predicting customer churn for a telecommunications company, an ensemble of models can offer more robust insights, and the agreement among the models contributes to interpretability.

3. **Hierarchical Models**

   – Explanation: Organizing models in a hierarchical structure to break down complex problems into more manageable subproblems.

   – Example: In supply chain optimization, a hierarchical model can address various aspects, such as inventory management, distribution, and demand forecasting, making the overall system more interpretable.

# Advanced Techniques for Interpretability

**Explainable AI (XAI)**

1. **SHAP Values**

   – Explanation: SHapley Additive exPlanations assign a value to each feature, indicating its contribution to a particular prediction.

   – Example code (Python—using SHAP library):

```python
import shap
explainer = shap.Explainer(model)
shap_values = explainer.shap_values(X_test)
shap.summary_plot(shap_values, X_test)
```

2. **Integrated Gradients**

   – Explanation: Measures the integral of the gradient of the model's prediction concerning the input features along a predefined path.

   – Example code (Python):

   ```python
   from captum.attr import IntegratedGradients
   ig = IntegratedGradients(model)
   attributions, _ = ig.attribute(inputs, target=0, return_convergence_delta=True)
   ```

3. **Counterfactual Explanations**

   – Explanation: Generates alternative scenarios by changing input features to observe the impact on predictions.

   – Example code (Python—using the "alibi" library):

   ```python
   from alibi.explainers import CounterFactual
   cf = CounterFactual(model, shape=(1,) + X_train.shape[1:])
   explanation = cf.explain(X_instance)
   ```

**Neural Network–Specific Techniques**

1. **Layer-Wise Relevance Propagation (LRP)**

   – Explanation: Distributes the relevance of the output across input features layer by layer, providing insights into feature contributions.

   – Example code (Python):

   ```python
   import investigate
   analyzer = investigate.create_analyzer("lrp.z", model)
   analysis = analyzer.analyze(X_sample)
   ```

2. **Attention Mechanisms**

   – Explanation: Visualizes attention weights, showing which parts of the input the model focuses on during processing.

   – Example code (Python—using TensorFlow and Keras):

```python
from tensorflow.keras.models import Model
attention_model = Model(inputs=model.input, outputs=model.
get_layer("attention_layer").output)
attention_weights = attention_model.predict(X_sample)
```

# Real-World Use Cases

**Finance: Fraud Detection**

1. Challenge:

   – Detecting fraudulent transactions with a complex AI model.

2. Solution:

   – Use ensemble models to combine predictions from different fraud detection algorithms.

   – Apply SHAP values to explain the contributions of specific transaction features to the final prediction.

3. Outcome:

   – Improved interpretability allows financial analysts to understand the rationale behind flagged transactions, aiding in decision-making and compliance.

**Healthcare: Disease Prediction**

1. Challenge:

   – Developing an interpretable AI model for predicting diseases from medical records.

2.  Solution:

    – Employ counterfactual explanations to generate alternative
      scenarios for patient records.

    – Implement sensitivity analysis to understand the impact of slight
      variations in patient data on predictions.

3.  Outcome:

    – Increased trust among healthcare professionals, leading to
      better-informed treatment decisions based on the model's
      explanations.

**Ecommerce: Product Recommendation**

1.  Challenge:

    – Building an interpretable AI model for product recommendations
      in an ecommerce platform.

2.  Solution:

    – Use hierarchical models to organize recommendation algorithms
      based on product categories.

    – Leverage feature importance analysis to highlight key factors
      influencing personalized recommendations.

3.  Outcome:

    – Enhanced user satisfaction as customers gain insights into why
      specific products are recommended, fostering trust in the recom-
      mendation system.

# Future Directions and Challenges

1.  **Explainability for Reinforcement Learning**

    – Trend: Developing interpretable models for reinforcement
      learning scenarios.

    – Example: In robotics, understanding why a robot makes specific
      decisions in dynamic environments is crucial for deployment
      and safety.

2. **Interactive Interpretability**

   – Trend: Creating interfaces that allow users to interactively explore and manipulate model explanations.

   – Example: In finance, analysts can tweak input variables in real time to observe how changes impact the model's predictions.

3. **Trade-Off Between Accuracy and Interpretability**

   – Challenge: Striking a balance between building highly accurate models and maintaining interpretability.

   – Consideration: As models become more complex, finding ways to simplify explanations without compromising accuracy remains a challenge.

4. **Scalability of Interpretability Techniques**

   – Challenge: Adapting interpretability techniques to handle the scale of data and model complexity in large-scale AI deployments.

   – Consideration: Ongoing research focuses on developing scalable techniques that provide meaningful insights without overwhelming computational resources.

Interpretability in scalable AI models is a critical aspect of the evolving AI landscape. Practices, strategies, and advanced techniques discussed here aim to demystify the decision-making processes of complex models. As AI continues to advance, the ability to interpret these models becomes not only a necessity for trust and accountability but also a driving force for responsible and ethical AI deployment across various industries. Balancing sophistication with transparency and interpretability ensures that AI remains a tool that augments human capabilities rather than a mysterious force. As we navigate the future of AI, the ongoing pursuit of interpretable models will shape a world where AI is not just powerful but also comprehensible and trustworthy.

# Privacy Considerations for Scalable AI Systems

As artificial intelligence (AI) systems become increasingly prevalent, the importance of safeguarding user privacy becomes paramount. Privacy considerations are particularly critical in scalable AI systems, where the potential impact on a large scale amplifies both benefits and risks.

## Foundational Principles

Principle 1: Data Minimization

Explanation: Limit the collection of personal data to only what is necessary for the intended purpose.

Example: Consider a scalable recommendation system. Instead of collecting a user's entire search history, focus only on relevant data points like recent searches or interactions.

Principle 2: Purpose Limitation

Explanation: Clearly define the purpose of collecting data and only use it for the specified purpose.

Example: In a scalable health monitoring system, data collected for tracking physical activity should not be repurposed for targeted advertising.

Principle 3: Consent Mechanisms

Explanation: Obtain explicit consent from users before collecting and using their data.

Example: When deploying a scalable AI-driven mobile app, include a clear consent dialogue that explains what data will be collected and for what purposes, allowing users to opt in or opt out.

## Technical Implementations

Implementation 1: Differential Privacy

Explanation: Differential privacy adds noise to individual data points to protect user privacy while still providing accurate aggregate information.

Example: In a scalable AI system analyzing user behavior for market trends, differential privacy ensures that individual user actions are indistinguishable in the aggregated results.

Implementation 2: Homomorphic Encryption

Explanation: Homomorphic encryption allows computation on encrypted data without decrypting it, preserving privacy during processing.

Example: In a scalable AI healthcare application, homomorphic encryption enables analyzing patient data without exposing sensitive information, ensuring privacy is maintained.

Implementation 3: Federated Learning

Explanation: Federated learning enables model training across decentralized devices without exchanging raw data, enhancing privacy.

Example: In a scalable AI system for predictive text on smartphones, the model improves based on user input without the need to send entire texts to a central server, preserving user privacy.

# Advanced Techniques

Technique 1: Synthetic Data Generation

Explanation: Generate artificial data that mimics real data, preserving statistical properties while removing identifiable information.

Example: In a scalable AI system for customer feedback analysis, synthetic data can be used for model training, eliminating the risk of exposing individual sentiments.

Technique 2: Secure Multi-Party Computation (SMPC)

Explanation: SMPC allows multiple parties to jointly compute a function over their inputs while keeping them private.

Example: In a scalable AI system for collaborative market research, companies can use SMPC to analyze combined data without sharing proprietary information.

Technique 3: Privacy-Preserving Machine Learning Models

Explanation: Train models in a way that protects sensitive information about individuals in the dataset.

Example: In a scalable AI system for personalized content recommendations, the model is designed to learn user preferences without storing explicit details about individual preferences.

# Use Cases and Examples

Use Case 1: Ecommerce Recommendation System

Example: A scalable ecommerce AI system recommends products based on user behavior. Privacy is maintained by only analyzing recent interactions, ensuring the system avoids unnecessary data collection.

Code snippet:

```python
Sample code for data collection in a privacy-conscious
recommendation system
user_data = get_recent_user_data(user_id)
recommendations = generate_recommendations(user_data)
```

Use Case 2: Health Monitoring App

Example: A scalable health monitoring app uses federated learning to improve its prediction models. Personal health data remains on users' devices, and the central server only receives aggregated insights.

Code snippet:

```python
Sample code for federated learning in a health monitoring app
model = initialize_model()
updated_model = federated_learning(model, user_devices)
```

Use Case 3: Market Research Platform

Example: A scalable market research AI platform uses SMPC to analyze data from multiple companies. Each company retains control over its proprietary data while contributing to the overall market trends.

Code snippet:

```python
Sample code for secure multi-party computation in a market research
platform
combined_results = secure_multi_party_computation(data_company_A, data_
company_B)
```

# Challenges and Solutions

Challenge 1: Balancing Utility and Privacy

Solution: Implement techniques like differential privacy to find the right balance between maintaining data utility for AI systems and preserving individual privacy.

Challenge 2: Regulatory Compliance

Solution: Stay informed about and adhere to data protection regulations such as GDPR or HIPAA, ensuring that scalable AI systems comply with legal standards.

Challenge 3: User Education and Transparency

Solution: Educate users about how their data will be used and provide transparent mechanisms for users to control their privacy settings within the AI system.

# Future Trends

Trend 1: Decentralized Identity Systems

Explanation: Decentralized identity systems enable users to have more control over their personal information, reducing reliance on centralized databases.

Example: A scalable social media AI platform uses decentralized identity systems, allowing users to manage and control access to their data.

Trend 2: Privacy-Preserving Analytics

Explanation: Advances in privacy-preserving analytics enable organizations to derive insights from data without compromising individual privacy.

Example: A scalable AI analytics tool allows companies to analyze trends in their customer base without accessing individual customer details.

Trend 3: Ethical AI Certification

Explanation: The emergence of ethical AI certifications ensures that scalable AI systems adhere to predefined ethical standards, providing users and regulators with confidence.

Example: An organization deploys a scalable AI system and obtains an ethical AI certification to demonstrate its commitment to user privacy and ethical practices.

In conclusion, ensuring privacy in scalable AI systems requires a holistic approach encompassing foundational principles, technical implementations, advanced techniques, real-world examples, and a proactive stance toward emerging trends. By incorporating privacy-centric practices, organizations can build AI systems that not only scale effectively but also respect and protect the privacy rights of individuals. As the AI landscape evolves, the ongoing commitment to privacy will be instrumental in fostering trust and responsible innovation.

# CHAPTER 10

# Case Studies and Best Practices

Artificial intelligence (AI) has evolved rapidly, transforming various industries with its innovative applications. However, implementing scalable AI systems can be challenging. In this chapter, we'll explore real-world case studies and best practices that shed light on successful strategies for deploying scalable AI solutions.

Before delving into case studies, it's essential to grasp the concept of scalability in AI. Scalability refers to a system's ability to handle increased workload or demand. In the context of AI, scalability involves designing systems that can efficiently accommodate growing datasets, increased computational requirements, and expanding user bases.

### Practice 1: Distributed Computing

Explanation:

Distributed computing involves breaking down complex tasks into smaller, manageable parts distributed across multiple servers or nodes. This practice is fundamental for scaling AI systems as it allows for parallel processing, enabling efficient utilization of resources.

Example:

Consider a speech recognition system that needs to process a vast amount of audio data. By distributing the workload across several servers, each handling a portion of the data, the overall processing time is significantly reduced.

Dask is a Python parallel computing framework intended for large-scale data calculations. It enables customers to smoothly scale their workflows from a single machine to clusters.

© Abhishek Mishra 2024
A. Mishra, *Scalable AI and Design Patterns*, https://doi.org/10.1007/979-8-8688-0158-7_10

Dask efficiently manages larger-than-memory datasets with dynamic task scheduling and parallelized processes. Dask is a vital tool for data scientists and developers dealing with massive data and difficult computations, as it integrates with prominent Python libraries and supports out-of-core computing, allowing users to leverage the full capacity of their computing resources.

**Algorithm Structure**

Load audio data.

Split the audio data into chunks.

Distribute the chunks to different servers or nodes.

Process each audio chunk in parallel.

Aggregate the processed results.

Output the final result.

Code snippet (Python—using Dask):

```python
import dask

@dask.delayed
def process_audio_chunk(chunk):
    Code to process audio chunk
    return processed_data

 Assuming audio_data is a large list of audio chunks
processed_results = [process_audio_chunk(chunk) for chunk in
audio_data]
final_result = dask.compute(*processed_results)
```

**Practice 2: Parallel Processing**

Explanation:

Parallel processing involves executing multiple tasks simultaneously, improving processing speed, and handling higher workloads effectively. In the context of AI, this is vital for tasks that can be broken down into parallelizable components.

Example:

In image recognition, parallel processing can be employed to analyze different sections of an image concurrently, allowing for faster and more efficient object detection.

**Algorithm Structure**

Load image data.

Divide the image into sections.

Create a pool of processes.

Distribute image sections to different processes.

Execute the processing function in parallel.

Collect and aggregate the results.

Output the final result.

Code snippet (Python—using multiprocessing):

```python
from multiprocessing import Pool

def process_image_section(section):
    Code to analyze image section
    return result

 Assuming image_sections is a list of image segments
with Pool() as pool:
    results = pool.map(process_image_section, image_sections)
```

**Practice 3: Adaptive Learning**

Explanation:

Adaptive learning involves creating AI models that can continuously learn and adapt to new data. This is essential for ensuring that AI systems remain relevant and accurate as they scale.

Example:

In a fraud detection system, adaptive learning allows the model to continuously update its understanding of fraudulent patterns based on new data, improving its detection capabilities over time.

**Algorithm Structure**

> Load training data and labels.
>
> Initialize the machine learning model (RandomForestClassifier).
>
> Train the model on the initial training data.
>
> Continuously update the model with new incoming data using partial_fit.
>
> Monitor model performance and update as needed.

Code snippet (Python—using scikit-learn):

```python
from sklearn.ensemble import RandomForestClassifier

 Assuming X_train, y_train are training data and labels
model = RandomForestClassifier()
model.fit(X_train, y_train)

 As new data becomes available
model.partial_fit(new_data, new_labels)
```

**Practice 4: Containerization**

Explanation:

Containerization involves packaging applications and their dependencies into containers, ensuring consistency and ease of deployment across different environments. This practice facilitates scalability by simplifying the process of managing and deploying AI applications.

Example:

Consider a natural language processing (NLP) application. Containerization allows the AI model and its dependencies to be encapsulated, making it easy to deploy the same model on various platforms without worrying about compatibility issues.

**Algorithm Structure**

Create a Dockerfile for the NLP application.

Define the base image (Python 3.8).

Copy the application code into the container.

Set the working directory.

Install application dependencies.

Specify the command to run the application.

Code snippet (Docker):

```dockerfile
 Dockerfile for an NLP application
FROM python:3.8

 Copy application code
COPY . /app

 Set working directory
WORKDIR /app

 Install dependencies
RUN pip install -r requirements.txt

 Command to run the application
CMD ["python", "app.py"]
```

**Practice 5: Auto-Scaling Infrastructure**

Explanation:

Auto-scaling infrastructure involves dynamically adjusting the computational resources based on the current workload. This ensures optimal resource utilization, especially during periods of high demand.

Example:

In a real-time translation service, auto-scaling infrastructure allows the system to automatically allocate more computational resources during peak usage times, ensuring low latency and a seamless user experience.

**Algorithm Structure**

Define the AWS CloudFormation template.

Specify the resources, for example, an Auto Scaling group.

Set properties such as minimum, maximum, and desired capacity.

Define scaling policies and triggers based on workload.

Deploy the CloudFormation template to provision resources.

Monitor system metrics.

Dynamically adjust the number of instances based on workload.

Code snippet (Infrastructure as Code—using AWS CloudFormation):

```yaml
Resources:
  MyAutoScalingGroup:
    Type: AWS::AutoScaling::AutoScalingGroup
    Properties:
      ...
      MinSize: 2
      MaxSize: 10
      DesiredCapacity: 2
      ...
```

# Advanced Techniques for Scalable AI

**Technique 1: Edge Computing**

Explanation:

Edge computing involves processing data closer to the source (edge devices) rather than relying solely on centralized cloud servers. This reduces latency and enhances scalability, making it particularly useful for AI applications requiring real-time responses.

Example:

In a smart home system with AI-powered security cameras, edge computing allows the cameras to process and analyze video data locally, reducing the need for constant communication with a central server.

Code snippet (TensorFlow Lite for edge devices):

```python
import tensorflow as tf
from tensorflow.lite.python.interpreter import Interpreter

 Load the TensorFlow Lite model
interpreter = Interpreter(model_content=model_content)
interpreter.allocate_tensors()

 Assuming input_data is the input for the model
interpreter.set_tensor(input_index, input_data)
interpreter.invoke()

 Retrieve the output
output_data = interpreter.get_tensor(output_index)
```

**Technique 2: Federated Learning**

Explanation:

Federated learning involves training machine learning models across decentralized devices while keeping data localized. This not only enhances scalability but also addresses privacy concerns associated with centralizing sensitive data.

Example:

In a healthcare scenario, federated learning allows hospitals to collaboratively train a disease prediction model without sharing patient data. Each hospital trains the model using its local data, and the global model is updated without centralized data storage.

Code snippet (PySyft for federated learning):

```python
import torch
import syft as sy

 Creating a virtual worker
hook = sy.TorchHook(torch)
worker = sy.VirtualWorker(hook, id="worker")

 Model training on remote data
model.send(worker)
optimizer = torch.optim.SGD(params=model.parameters(), lr=0.01)

for epoch in range(epochs):
    for data, target in remote_data:
         Forward pass, backward pass, and optimization
        model = model.send(data.location)
        optimizer.zero_grad()
        output = model(data)
        loss = criterion(output, target)
        loss.backward()
        optimizer.step()
```

# Case Study: Uber's Scalable AI Infrastructure

Background:

Uber, a pioneer in the ride-sharing industry, relies heavily on AI for various aspects of its platform, including route optimization, demand prediction, and fraud detection. As Uber expanded globally, the need for a scalable AI infrastructure became paramount.

**Strategies and Practices**

1. **Distributed Computing**: Uber utilizes a distributed computing framework to process vast amounts of ride and location data efficiently. By distributing tasks across multiple servers, they can handle the dynamic nature of ride requests and optimize routes in real time.

2. **Auto-Scaling Infrastructure**: During peak hours or in high-demand areas, Uber's auto-scaling infrastructure dynamically adjusts the number of servers and computational resources. This ensures that the AI algorithms for ride matching and surge pricing can handle the increased workload without compromising performance.

3. **Edge Computing**: Uber employs edge computing for some AI applications, particularly in the context of driver assistance and safety features. Edge devices in vehicles can process data locally, enabling faster decision-making and reducing dependence on constant communication with central servers.

4. **Federated Learning for Fraud Detection**: To enhance fraud detection without compromising user privacy, Uber employs federated learning. Each region trains its fraud detection model on local data, and the global model is updated collaboratively. This ensures that the system scales globally while respecting data privacy regulations.

5. **Containerization for AI Models**: Uber uses containerization to deploy and manage AI models across different components of its platform. This ensures consistency in model deployment, making it easier to scale AI applications seamlessly across diverse environments.

# Lessons Learned

Uber's case highlights the importance of a holistic approach to scalability. By combining distributed computing, auto-scaling infrastructure, edge computing, federated learning, and containerization, Uber has built a robust AI infrastructure capable of handling the complex and dynamic demands of the ride-sharing industry on a global scale.

Implementing scalable AI solutions is a multifaceted challenge that requires a combination of practices and advanced techniques. Real-world case studies, such as those explored in this discussion, provide valuable insights into the strategies adopted by industry leaders like Netflix, Google, Amazon, and Uber. From distributed computing and parallel processing to adaptive learning and containerization, these practices form the foundation of scalable AI systems.

As technology continues to evolve, advanced techniques like edge computing and federated learning are becoming increasingly crucial. The provided examples and code snippets offer a practical understanding of how these techniques can be implemented in real-world scenarios.

In conclusion, a nuanced and strategic approach to scalability, informed by real-world case studies and leveraging advanced techniques, is essential for organizations seeking to harness the full potential of AI in an ever-expanding landscape.

Certainly! Let's dive deeper into real-world examples that illustrate the implementation of scalable AI solutions using the practices and advanced techniques discussed earlier.

# Real-World Examples

1. **Distributed Computing: Google's PageRank Algorithm**

    Background:

    Google's search engine processes an enormous amount of web pages to deliver relevant results. PageRank, Google's algorithm for ranking web pages, is an excellent example of distributed computing.

    Implementation:

    Google breaks down the task of ranking web pages into smaller components distributed across its vast server network. Each server processes a subset of web pages, and the results are combined to produce the overall page rankings.

    Impact:

    By using distributed computing, Google ensures that its search algorithm scales efficiently with the ever-growing size of the Internet, providing users with relevant and timely search results.

2. **Parallel Processing: Image Classification at Scale**

Background:

Image classification tasks, such as identifying objects in images, often require analyzing large datasets. Parallel processing is crucial for accelerating these tasks.

Implementation:

Companies like Pinterest employ parallel processing to categorize and recommend images to users. Multiple servers process different images simultaneously, improving the speed and scalability of image classification.

Impact:

Pinterest can efficiently handle the vast number of images uploaded by users, ensuring a seamless and quick image recommendation experience for its user base.

3. **Adaptive Learning: Netflix Recommendation System**

Background:

Netflix's recommendation system is a classic example of adaptive learning, where the system continuously learns and adapts to user preferences.

Implementation:

Netflix analyzes user viewing habits, ratings, and interactions with the platform to tailor content recommendations. As user preferences evolve, the recommendation algorithm adapts to provide personalized suggestions.

Impact:

The adaptive learning approach enhances user satisfaction and retention by offering a personalized content catalog, contributing to Netflix's success as a leading streaming platform.

4.  **Containerization: OpenAI's GPT Models**

Background:

OpenAI's Generative Pretrained Transformer (GPT) models, such as GPT-3, are powerful language models used for a variety of natural language processing tasks.

Implementation:

OpenAI utilizes containerization to deploy and manage GPT models. Containerized models can be easily scaled across different platforms and integrated into various applications, ensuring consistent performance.

Impact:

Containerization simplifies the deployment process, allowing developers to integrate GPT models seamlessly into diverse environments, from chatbots to content generation applications.

5.  **Auto-Scaling Infrastructure: Amazon Web Services (AWS)**

Background:

AWS, one of the leading cloud service providers, employs auto-scaling infrastructure to accommodate varying workloads for its clients.

Implementation:

AWS allows users to set up auto-scaling configurations, enabling resources to automatically adjust based on demand. This is particularly useful for AI applications hosted on AWS, ensuring optimal performance during peak usage periods.

Impact:

Auto-scaling infrastructure on AWS ensures that AI applications hosted on the platform can efficiently handle fluctuations in demand, optimizing resource utilization and cost-effectiveness.

6. **Edge Computing: Tesla's Autopilot**

Background:

Tesla's Autopilot system relies on AI for autonomous driving capabilities, and edge computing plays a crucial role in processing data from sensors in real time.

Implementation:

Edge devices within Tesla vehicles process data from cameras, sensors, and radar locally. This enables rapid decision-making for tasks like object detection and path planning without relying solely on a centralized server.

Impact:

Edge computing in Tesla's Autopilot system reduces latency, enhances real-time decision-making, and contributes to the overall safety and efficiency of autonomous driving.

7. **Federated Learning: Apple's Siri**

Background:

Apple's Siri, a virtual assistant powered by AI, uses federated learning to improve language understanding and user experience.

Implementation:

Siri employs federated learning to enhance its language models. Each user's device trains a local model on personalized language data, and the global model is updated collaboratively without centralizing individual user data.

Impact:

Federated learning in Siri ensures that the virtual assistant becomes more personalized and accurate without compromising user privacy, contributing to a better user experience.

8.  **Distributed Computing in Climate Modeling: European Centre for Medium-Range Weather Forecasts (ECMWF)**

    Background:

    The ECMWF uses advanced climate models to predict weather patterns and provide medium-range weather forecasts globally.

    Implementation:

    To handle the complexity of climate modeling, ECMWF employs distributed computing. The massive computational workload is distributed across multiple high-performance servers, allowing for the parallel processing of vast datasets.

    Impact:

    Distributed computing enables ECMWF to run intricate simulations, improving the accuracy and scope of weather forecasts. This has far-reaching implications for disaster preparedness, agriculture, and various industries dependent on weather predictions.

9.  **Parallel Processing in Drug Discovery: IBM's Summit Supercomputer**

    Background:

    Drug discovery involves analyzing vast datasets to identify potential compounds for pharmaceutical development.

    Implementation:

    IBM's Summit supercomputer, one of the most powerful in the world, employs parallel processing to accelerate drug discovery. Multiple processors work simultaneously to analyze complex biological data, significantly speeding up the drug discovery pipeline.

Impact:

Parallel processing in drug discovery helps researchers sift through immense datasets, accelerating the identification of potential drug candidates. This has implications for developing treatments for various diseases, including cancer and infectious diseases.

10. **Adaptive Learning in Personalized Healthcare: Google's DeepMind Health**

Background:

DeepMind Health, a subsidiary of Google's DeepMind, focuses on applying AI to healthcare challenges.

Implementation:

DeepMind Health utilizes adaptive learning to create personalized healthcare models. For instance, in the case of predicting patient deterioration, the models continuously learn from patient data, adapting to individual medical histories and evolving conditions.

Impact:

Adaptive learning in healthcare AI models contributes to personalized treatment plans and early detection of medical issues, ultimately improving patient outcomes and reducing the strain on healthcare resources.

11. **Containerization for AI in Financial Services: JPMorgan Chase**

Background:

Financial institutions deal with vast amounts of data for risk assessment, fraud detection, and customer interactions.

Implementation:

JPMorgan Chase employs containerization for deploying AI models in its financial services. This allows for consistent deployment across various departments and applications, ensuring that AI-powered insights are seamlessly integrated into the organization's operations.

Impact:

Containerization streamlines the deployment of AI applications in the financial sector, enhancing the efficiency of risk management, fraud prevention, and customer service.

12. **Auto-Scaling Infrastructure in Social Media: Facebook's Content Moderation**

Background:

Social media platforms like Facebook process an immense volume of user-generated content, requiring scalable AI for content moderation.

Implementation:

Facebook utilizes auto-scaling infrastructure to handle fluctuations in content moderation demands. During periods of increased user activity, the computational resources dedicated to content moderation automatically scale to maintain efficient processing.

Impact:

Auto-scaling infrastructure ensures that content moderation remains effective even during peak usage times, fostering a safer and more reliable social media experience.

13. **Edge Computing in Healthcare IoT: Philips Healthcare**

Background:

Healthcare IoT devices generate a continuous stream of patient data that needs to be processed in real time.

Implementation:

Philips Healthcare integrates edge computing into its IoT devices, allowing for local processing of patient data at the point of care. This reduces latency in critical healthcare applications, such as patient monitoring and diagnostics.

Impact:

Edge computing in healthcare IoT devices contributes to timely decision-making, enhances patient care, and ensures that healthcare professionals have immediate access to relevant information.

14. **Federated Learning in Financial Fraud Detection: Mastercard**

Background:

Financial institutions face constant threats of fraud, requiring advanced solutions for detection.

Implementation:

Mastercard employs federated learning for fraud detection. Each financial institution in the network trains its local model on transaction data, and the global model is updated collaboratively. This approach enhances fraud detection without compromising sensitive transaction details.

Impact:

Federated learning in financial fraud detection enables a collective defense against evolving fraud patterns while respecting privacy and compliance regulations.

These real-world examples showcase the diverse applications of scalable AI solutions, from weather forecasting and drug discovery to personalized healthcare and financial services. The strategies and techniques discussed earlier are not isolated concepts but practical approaches that organizations across various industries leverage to harness the power of AI at scale.

15. **Distributed Computing in Astrophysics: Square Kilometre Array (SKA) Telescope**

Background:

The SKA telescope, a next-generation radio telescope, is designed to explore the universe by capturing vast amounts of radio signals.

Implementation:

To process the immense volume of data collected by SKA, distributed computing is crucial. The data is distributed across multiple processing units, enabling astronomers to analyze radio signals from different parts of the sky concurrently.

Impact:

Distributed computing allows SKA to unravel the mysteries of the universe efficiently, enabling astronomers to study cosmic phenomena and conduct groundbreaking research in astrophysics.

16. **Parallel Processing in Oil and Gas Exploration: Chevron's High-Performance Computing Center**

Background:

Oil and gas exploration involves analyzing seismic data to locate potential reserves beneath the Earth's surface.

Implementation:

Chevron's High-Performance Computing Center employs parallel processing to accelerate seismic data processing. Multiple processors work simultaneously to interpret and analyze seismic data, improving the accuracy of subsurface imaging.

Impact:

Parallel processing enhances the speed and efficiency of oil and gas exploration, allowing companies like Chevron to make informed decisions about resource extraction and reservoir management.

17. **Adaptive Learning for Speech Recognition: Apple's Siri and Google Assistant**

Background:

Voice-activated virtual assistants, such as Siri and Google Assistant, rely on speech recognition technology.

Implementation:

Adaptive learning is applied to continuously improve the accuracy of speech recognition. As users interact with these virtual assistants, the systems adapt to individual speech patterns, accents, and language nuances.

Impact:

Adaptive learning in speech recognition enhances the user experience, making virtual assistants more adept at understanding and responding to diverse linguistic inputs.

18. **Containerization in Ecommerce Recommendation Systems: Shopify**

Background:

Ecommerce platforms utilize recommendation systems to enhance customer experience and drive sales.

Implementation:

Shopify employs containerization to deploy recommendation algorithms across its ecommerce platform consistently. Containerized applications ensure that the recommendation engine functions seamlessly regardless of the specific online store's configuration.

Impact:

Containerization streamlines the integration of recommendation systems into various online stores, contributing to personalized shopping experiences for users.

19. **Auto-Scaling Infrastructure in Online Gaming: Epic Games (*Fortnite*)**

Background:

Online gaming platforms experience varying levels of user activity, especially during events and updates.

Implementation:

Epic Games uses auto-scaling infrastructure for its popular game, *Fortnite*. During peak times, such as game launches or special events, the infrastructure dynamically adjusts to handle the increased number of players and maintain a smooth gaming experience.

Impact:

Auto-scaling infrastructure ensures that *Fortnite* can accommodate millions of players simultaneously, delivering a seamless and enjoyable gaming experience.

20. **Edge Computing in Smart Cities: Barcelona's Smart Lighting System**

Background:

Smart city initiatives involve deploying IoT devices for various applications, including intelligent lighting systems.
Implementation:

Barcelona's smart lighting system utilizes edge computing to process data from sensors embedded in streetlights locally. This allows for real-time adjustments to lighting conditions based on factors such as traffic flow and weather.

Impact:

Edge computing in smart lighting systems enhances energy efficiency, reduces latency, and contributes to the overall sustainability of urban environments.

These additional examples demonstrate the wide-ranging applications of scalable AI solutions across different industries, from astronomy and oil exploration to virtual assistants, ecommerce, gaming, and smart city initiatives. Each example showcases the practical implementation of strategies and advanced techniques discussed earlier, underscoring the versatility and impact of scalable AI in diverse domains.

# Understanding the Importance of Scalability in AI

Scalability in the context of AI involves designing systems that can handle growing datasets, increased computational demands, and expanding user bases. A scalable AI system ensures that it can efficiently adapt to changes in workload and data volume without compromising performance. To achieve this, several best practices and strategies need to be incorporated into the design and implementation process.

## Best Practices for Scalable AI Systems

1. **Distributed Computing**

   Explanation: Distributing computational tasks across multiple servers or nodes to enhance performance and handle increased workloads efficiently.

   Example: Consider a recommendation system for an ecommerce platform. By employing distributed computing, the system can process user preferences and generate recommendations concurrently, ensuring timely and responsive results.

   Code example (Python with Apache Spark):

   ```python
   from pyspark import SparkContext

   sc = SparkContext("local", "DistributedComputingExample")
   data = [1, 2, 3, 4, 5, 6, 7, 8, 9, 10]
   distributed_data = sc.parallelize(data)
   result = distributed_data.map(lambda x: x * 2).collect()
   print(result)
   ```

2. **Parallel Processing**

   Explanation: Executing multiple tasks simultaneously to enhance processing speed and handle higher workloads.

   Example: In natural language processing, parallel processing can be applied to analyze multiple documents concurrently, significantly reducing the time required for tasks like sentiment analysis.

Code example (Python with multiprocessing):

```python
from multiprocessing import Pool

def process_document(document):
    Perform NLP tasks on the document
    return processed_data

documents = [doc1, doc2, doc3, ...]
with Pool(processes=4) as pool:
    results = pool.map(process_document, documents)
```

3. **Auto-Scaling Infrastructure**

   Explanation: Automatically adjust the computational resources based on the current workload to optimize efficiency.

   Example: In a cloud-based AI application, auto-scaling allows the system to dynamically allocate more resources during periods of high demand and scale down during periods of low activity.

   Code example (AWS Auto Scaling):

```python
 AWS SDK for Python (Boto3) example
import boto3

client = boto3.client('autoscaling')
response = client.update_auto_scaling_group(
    AutoScalingGroupName='your-auto-scaling-group',
    MinSize=2,
    MaxSize=10,
    DesiredCapacity=5
)
```

4. **Containerization**

   Explanation: Packaging applications and their dependencies into containers for easy deployment and scalability.

   Example: Containerizing a machine learning model allows for seamless deployment across different environments, ensuring consistent behavior and easy scalability.

   Code example (Docker):

   ```Dockerfile
   FROM python:3.8

   COPY requirements.txt /app/
   RUN pip install --no-cache-dir -r /app/requirements.txt

   COPY . /app/
   WORKDIR /app/

   CMD ["python", "your_ml_model.py"]
   ```

5. **Adaptive Learning**

   Explanation: Developing AI models that can learn and adapt to new data, ensuring continuous improvement and relevance.

   Example: In fraud detection, an adaptive learning model can evolve to recognize new patterns of fraudulent behavior, enhancing its accuracy over time.

   Code example (scikit-learn—online learning):

   ```python
   from sklearn.linear_model import SGDClassifier

   model = SGDClassifier(loss='log', max_iter=1000)
   for batch in training_data:
       X_batch, y_batch = preprocess_data(batch)
       model.partial_fit(X_batch, y_batch, classes=[0, 1])
   ```

# Advanced Techniques for Scalable AI Systems

1. **Edge Computing**

   Explanation: Processing data closer to the source (edge devices) to reduce latency and enhance scalability.

   Example: In image recognition, edge computing can be applied to process images on the device itself, reducing the need for extensive data transfer and enabling real-time analysis.

   Code example (TensorFlow Lite for edge devices):

   ```python
   import tensorflow as tf
   interpreter = tf.lite.Interpreter(model_content=tflite_model)
   interpreter.allocate_tensors()
   ```

2. **Federated Learning**

   Explanation: Training machine learning models across decentralized devices while keeping data localized, improving scalability and privacy.

   Example: In healthcare, federated learning enables collaborative model training across different hospitals without sharing patient data.

   Code example (PySyft for federated learning):

   ```python
   import torch
   import syft

   hook = syft.TorchHook(torch)
   client = syft.VirtualWorker(hook, id="client")
   server = syft.VirtualWorker(hook, id="server")

   model = ...   Define your model
   ```

```
Federated learning loop
for epoch in range(num_epochs):
    model = model.send(client)
    updated_model = train(model, client_data)
    model = updated_model.get()
    model = model.send(server)
```

# Use Cases and Real-World Examples

1. **Google's BERT for Natural Language Processing**

   Use case: Google's BERT (Bidirectional Encoder Representations from Transformers) is a pretrained natural language processing model that has been scaled effectively for various applications such as sentiment analysis and question answering.

2. **Uber's Michelangelo for Machine Learning Orchestration**

   Use case: Uber's Michelangelo platform orchestrates machine learning models at scale, handling tasks such as model training, deployment, and monitoring in a distributed and scalable manner.

3. **Facebook's Prophet for Time Series Forecasting**

   Use case: Facebook's Prophet is a scalable tool for time series forecasting that allows businesses to predict future trends, making it widely applicable in finance, supply chain management, and resource planning.

# Challenges and Mitigations

1. **Data Privacy and Security**

   Challenge: Ensuring the privacy and security of user data becomes more complex as systems scale.

   Mitigation: Implementing robust encryption, access controls, and compliance with data protection regulations.

191

2.  **Resource Management**

Challenge: Efficiently managing computational resources as the system scales can be challenging.

Mitigation: Utilizing cloud services, advanced resource orchestration tools, and monitoring systems for dynamic resource allocation.

# Continuous Monitoring and Optimization

1.  **Performance Monitoring**

Importance: Regularly monitoring system performance is crucial for identifying bottlenecks and areas that require optimization.

Strategy: Implement tools for real-time monitoring of resource usage, response times, and error rates to ensure the system operates within defined performance thresholds.

Example: Using Prometheus and Grafana to monitor key metrics such as CPU utilization, memory usage, and response times in a scalable AI system.

Code example (Prometheus metrics in Python):

```python
```python
from prometheus_client import start_http_server, Summary
import random
import time

 Define a metric
REQUEST_TIME = Summary('request_processing_seconds', 'Time
spent processing request')

 Decorate your function with the metric
@REQUEST_TIME.time()
def process_request():
    time.sleep(random.random())
```
```

```
    Start the Prometheus server
if __name__ == '__main__':
    start_http_server(8000)
    while True:
        process_request()
```

2. **Dynamic Resource Allocation**

   Importance: Dynamically adjusting resources based on demand
   optimizes costs and ensures efficient utilization.

   Strategy: Employ auto-scaling policies and algorithms that adapt
   to changing workloads, scaling resources up or down as needed.

   Example: Implementing Kubernetes Horizontal Pod Autoscaler
   (HPA) to automatically adjust the number of running pods based
   on resource usage.

   Code example (Kubernetes HPA configuration):

```yaml
apiVersion: autoscaling/v2
kind: HorizontalPodAutoscaler
metadata:
  name: your-hpa
spec:
  scaleTargetRef:
    apiVersion: apps/v1
    kind: Deployment
    name: your-deployment
  minReplicas: 2
  maxReplicas: 10
  metrics:
    - type: Resource
      resource:
        name: cpu
        targetAverageUtilization: 80
```

# Advanced Data Management

1. **Data Partitioning**

   Importance: Efficiently managing large datasets by partitioning them based on specific criteria improves data retrieval and processing times.

   Strategy: Partition data based on relevant attributes (e.g., user ID, timestamp) to distribute the workload evenly across the system. Example: Partitioning a user activity log based on user IDs to enable parallel processing and quicker access to user-specific data.

   Code example (SQL table partitioning):

   ```sql
   CREATE TABLE user_activity (
       user_id INT,
       activity_date DATE,
       activity_type VARCHAR(255),
       -- Other columns
   )
   PARTITION BY RANGE (user_id) (
       PARTITION p0 VALUES LESS THAN (1000),
       PARTITION p1 VALUES LESS THAN (2000),
       PARTITION p2 VALUES LESS THAN (MAXVALUE)
   );
   ```

2. **Data Caching**

   Importance: Minimizing redundant computations by caching frequently used data can significantly improve response times.

   Strategy: Implement a caching layer that stores and retrieves results from frequently executed queries or computations. Example: Using Redis as an in-memory cache for storing frequently accessed model predictions in a recommendation system.

Code example (Python with Redis):

```python
import redis

 Connect to Redis
r = redis.StrictRedis(host='localhost', port=6379, db=0)

 Cache the result of a function
def expensive_computation(key):
    if not (result := r.get(key)):
        result = perform_expensive_computation()
        r.setex(key, result, 3600)   Cache for one hour
    return result
```

# Decentralized Processing with Microservices

1. **Microservices Architecture**

   Importance: Breaking down the monolithic structure into smaller, independent microservices facilitates scalability, maintainability, and deployment flexibility.

   Strategy: Design individual microservices responsible for specific tasks, enabling independent scaling and deployment.
   Example: Decomposing a large AI application into microservices such as user authentication, recommendation engine, and data processing.

   Code example (Python with Flask—microservice API):

   ```python
   from flask import Flask, jsonify

   app = Flask(__name__)

   @app.route('/recommendation', methods=['GET'])
   def get_recommendation():
        Logic for recommendation
       return jsonify({'recommendation': 'your_recommendation'})
   ```

```python
if __name__ == '__main__':
    app.run(port=5000)
```

# DevOps Integration for Seamless Deployment

1. **Continuous Integration and Deployment (CI/CD)**

   Importance: Automating the integration, testing, and deployment processes ensures a streamlined and error-free delivery pipeline.

   Strategy: Implement CI/CD pipelines to automatically build, test, and deploy AI applications, reducing manual errors and improving deployment speed.

   Example: Utilizing Jenkins for orchestrating a CI/CD pipeline that automates testing and deployment processes.

   Code example (Jenkins Pipeline script):

```groovy
pipeline {
    agent any

    stages {
        stage('Build') {
            steps {
                script {
                    // Build your application
                }
            }
        }
        stage('Test') {
            steps {
                script {
                    // Run tests
                }
            }
        }
```

```
stage('Deploy') {
    steps {
        script {
            // Deploy to production
        }
    }
}
    }
}
```

In the rapidly evolving landscape of AI, designing and implementing scalable systems is paramount for success. Continuous monitoring, dynamic resource allocation, advanced data management, decentralized processing with microservices, and DevOps integration collectively form a robust framework for building scalable AI systems. Real-world examples and code snippets provide practical insights into applying these best practices and advanced strategies.

As organizations embrace the challenges of scalability, incorporating these practices into their AI development processes will not only ensure efficient and responsive systems but also position them at the forefront of technological innovation. The journey to scalable AI systems is an ongoing process, and staying abreast of emerging technologies and industry trends will contribute to the sustained success of AI applications in diverse domains.

Building scalable AI systems is a multifaceted endeavor that demands a strategic and holistic approach. The integration of distributed computing, parallel processing, auto-scaling infrastructure, containerization, and adaptive learning can provide a robust foundation for scalability. Advanced techniques like edge computing and federated learning further enhance the capabilities of AI systems, addressing specific challenges in latency and data privacy.

By understanding these best practices, strategies, and advanced techniques, organizations can embark on the journey of designing and implementing scalable AI systems with confidence. The use cases and real-world examples illustrate how these practices are applied in diverse domains, contributing to the successful deployment of AI solutions that can evolve and adapt to the ever-changing landscape of technology.

Real-world examples demonstrate the practical implementation of scalable AI solutions in diverse domains, from search engines and streaming platforms to autonomous vehicles and virtual assistants. The strategies and advanced techniques discussed earlier are not merely theoretical; they are integral to the success of industry leaders who have effectively harnessed the power of AI at scale.

Understanding how these practices are applied in real-world scenarios provides valuable insights for organizations aiming to develop and deploy scalable AI solutions. The landscape of AI is dynamic, and as technology advances, the lessons learned from these examples will continue to shape the future of scalable AI applications.

# CHAPTER 11

# Future Trends and Emerging Technologies

The field of artificial intelligence (AI) is undergoing rapid transformations, with emerging technologies and trends poised to reshape the landscape of scalable AI. In this chapter, we delve into ten key trends and technologies that will play pivotal roles in the future of AI, exploring their implications and real-world applications.

## Emerging Trend: Generative AI

Explanation:

Generative AI is a transformative technology that involves systems capable of creating, imitating, or enhancing content. It plays a pivotal role in the future of AI, contributing to advancements in creativity, xsolving.

## Real-World Applications

### Medicine

**Drug Discovery**: Generative AI assists in designing new drug compounds by predicting molecular structures with desired properties. This accelerates the drug discovery process, potentially leading to the development of more effective treatments.

**Medical Imaging Enhancement**: Generative models enhance medical images, providing clearer visuals for diagnostics. This aids healthcare professionals in making accurate assessments and improves patient care.

© Abhishek Mishra 2024
A. Mishra, *Scalable AI and Design Patterns*, https://doi.org/10.1007/979-8-8688-0158-7_11

### Fintech

**Fraud Detection**: Generative AI generates synthetic data for training robust fraud detection models. By simulating a wide range of fraudulent scenarios, it improves the model's ability to detect and prevent fraudulent activities effectively.

**Algorithmic Trading Strategies**: Generative models analyze historical market data to generate new algorithmic trading strategies. This optimization enhances decision-making processes in the financial industry, contributing to more efficient trading.

### Creativity

**Artistic Content Generation**: Generative AI creates realistic artworks, designs, and multimedia content. This technology serves as a valuable tool for artists and designers, providing inspiration and assistance in the creative process.

**Music Composition**: AI-driven generative models compose original music, collaborating with human musicians to produce unique and innovative compositions. This expands the possibilities in music creation and exploration.

### Productivity

**Content Creation and Copywriting**: Generative AI assists in generating written content, including articles, marketing copy, and code snippets. This automation frees up time for professionals, allowing them to focus on higher-level tasks and strategic aspects of their work.

**Automated Design**: Generative design tools powered by AI automate the creation of product prototypes. These tools optimize designs based on specified parameters and constraints, streamlining the product development process.

Generative AI is a versatile technology with far-reaching implications across diverse industries, fostering innovation and efficiency in various applications. Its ability to create and enhance content opens up new possibilities for addressing complex challenges and driving advancements in multiple domains.

Other key trends are

1. **Explainable AI (XAI)**

   Overview:

   Explainable AI focuses on making AI systems more transparent and understandable. As AI algorithms become more complex, there is a growing need to interpret and explain their decisions, especially in critical domains such as healthcare, finance, and justice.

Example:

In a healthcare setting, an XAI model can provide clear explanations for diagnostic decisions, aiding medical professionals in understanding the reasoning behind a particular diagnosis or treatment recommendation.

2.  **Federated Learning**

Overview:

Federated learning is a decentralized training approach where machine learning models are trained across multiple devices without exchanging raw data. This ensures privacy and allows models to be trained collaboratively without centralizing sensitive information.

Example:

Consider a predictive keyboard on a smartphone. Federated learning enables the model to learn from the user's typing patterns on the device itself, without sending personal data to a central server, preserving user privacy.

3.  **Edge Computing in AI**

Overview:

Edge computing involves processing data closer to the source, reducing latency, and enabling real-time processing. In AI, this means running algorithms on local devices or servers rather than relying solely on centralized cloud servers.

Example:

In a smart city scenario, edge computing allows AI systems to process data from sensors in real time, enabling quick decision-making for tasks such as traffic management and emergency response.

### 4.   Human Augmentation

Overview:

Human augmentation involves integrating AI technologies with the human body to enhance physical and cognitive abilities. This trend explores the synergies between humans and machines, opening new frontiers in healthcare, industry, and daily life.

Example:

In a manufacturing setting, workers equipped with exoskeletons powered by AI can enhance their strength and endurance, reducing the risk of physical strain and injuries.

### 5.   Quantum Computing

Overview:

Quantum computing leverages the principles of quantum mechanics to perform computations at speeds unimaginable by classical computers. In scalable AI, quantum computing holds the potential to accelerate complex calculations and model training.

Example:

For financial institutions, quantum computing can optimize portfolio management by quickly analyzing vast datasets and simulating various market scenarios, leading to more informed investment decisions.

### 6.   Neuromorphic Computing

Overview:

Neuromorphic computing mimics the architecture and functionality of the human brain, using artificial neurons for more efficient and brain-like information processing.

Example:

In autonomous vehicles, neuromorphic computing allows the system to learn and adapt to complex traffic scenarios, improving decision-making in real time and enhancing overall safety.

7. **Bio-Inspired AI**

Overview:

Bio-inspired AI draws inspiration from biological systems to design intelligent algorithms. This approach seeks to replicate the adaptive, resilient, and efficient nature of living organisms.

Example:
In agriculture, bio-inspired AI can optimize crop management by mimicking the behavior of ecosystems, leading to sustainable farming practices and improved crop yields.

8. **AI in Generative Design**

Overview:

Generative design uses AI algorithms to create and optimize designs based on specified criteria. This technology applies not only to static objects but also to dynamic systems, offering innovative solutions in various domains.

Example:

Architects using AI in generative design can input constraints and preferences for a building project. The AI then generates multiple design options, considering factors like structural integrity, energy efficiency, and aesthetic appeal.

9. **Autonomous Systems and Robotics**

Overview:

Autonomous systems and robotics involve the integration of AI to enable machines to operate independently and make decisions in dynamic environments.

Example:

In logistics, autonomous drones equipped with AI can efficiently navigate warehouses, manage inventory, and optimize the picking and packing processes, enhancing overall operational efficiency.

10. **AI-Powered Personalization**

Overview:

AI-powered personalization utilizes machine learning algorithms to tailor products, services, and content to individual preferences, providing a personalized user experience.

Example:

Streaming platforms use AI-powered personalization to recommend movies or music based on a user's viewing or listening history, creating a more engaging and customized content consumption experience.

# Implications of Future Trends and Emerging Technologies

1. **Ethical Considerations**

As AI becomes more integrated into society, ethical considerations become paramount. Transparency in explainable AI addresses concerns related to biased decision-making, ensuring fair and accountable AI systems.

2. **Privacy and Security Challenges**

Decentralized approaches like federated learning and edge computing raise concerns about data privacy and security. Striking a balance between utilizing personal data for model improvement and protecting user privacy is crucial.

3. **Accessibility and Inclusivity**

Ensuring that the benefits of scalable AI are accessible to diverse populations is essential. It requires considering the needs of different communities and avoiding biases in AI systems, promoting inclusivity and equitable access to AI technologies.

4. **Skill Development and Education**

The rapid evolution of AI technologies necessitates continuous skill development. There is a growing need for education and training programs that equip individuals with the knowledge and skills to understand, develop, and manage these advanced AI systems.

The future of scalable AI is marked by a convergence of diverse trends and emerging technologies. From explainable AI to quantum computing, each trend brings unique opportunities and challenges. Navigating this future requires a holistic approach that considers ethical implications, addresses privacy concerns, promotes inclusivity, and fosters ongoing education. By embracing these principles, we can harness the full potential of scalable AI for the betterment of society.

# Advancements in Cloud Computing for Scalable AI

Cloud computing has become the backbone of scalable AI, providing the infrastructure and resources needed to process vast amounts of data and train complex models. From practices and strategies to cutting-edge techniques, we'll unravel the intricacies of this dynamic intersection.

# The Foundation: Cloud Computing in AI

Cloud **computing** involves the delivery of computing services—such as storage, processing power, and applications—over the Internet. This model allows organizations to access and utilize resources without the need for extensive physical infrastructure. In the context of AI, cloud computing provides the flexibility and scalability required for handling the computational demands of machine learning and deep learning.

# Practices and Strategies for Scalable AI in the Cloud

1. **Elasticity and Auto-Scaling**

   Overview:

   Elasticity and auto-scaling are strategies that enable AI systems to adapt to changing workloads by automatically adjusting the resources allocated based on demand.

   Implementation:

   In cloud environments, tools like AWS Auto Scaling or Google Cloud's Instance Groups can be configured to monitor system load. As demand increases, these tools automatically provision additional resources, ensuring optimal performance without manual intervention.

   Example:

   Consider a retail website that uses AI for demand forecasting. During peak shopping seasons, elasticity and auto-scaling ensure that the AI models have sufficient computational resources to handle the increased demand for predictions.

2. **Serverless Computing**

   Overview:

   Serverless computing allows developers to focus on writing code without managing the underlying infrastructure. Resources are allocated dynamically in response to events, minimizing operational overhead.

   Implementation:

   Cloud providers offer serverless platforms, such as AWS Lambda or Azure Functions, where developers can deploy AI functions without provisioning or managing servers. This pay-as-you-go model aligns costs with actual usage.

Example:

A sentiment analysis application using serverless computing can automatically scale based on the volume of incoming data, processing user feedback in real time without the need for constant resource management.

3. **Distributed Computing**

Overview:

Distributed computing involves breaking down a task into smaller subtasks that can be processed independently. This strategy enhances parallelism and accelerates computation.

Implementation:

Frameworks like Apache Spark or Dask enable distributed computing in the cloud. These frameworks distribute data and computations across multiple nodes, speeding up tasks like large-scale data processing or training machine learning models.

Example:

A healthcare organization analyzing a massive dataset of patient records for research purposes can leverage distributed computing to expedite data processing and gain insights more efficiently.

4. **Data Management and Storage Strategies**

Overview:

Efficient data management and storage are critical for scalable AI. Cloud-based data warehouses and object storage solutions are common components of a robust infrastructure.

Implementation:

Cloud services like Amazon S3 or Google Cloud Storage provide scalable, durable, and secure storage for large datasets. Data lakes, built on platforms like AWS Lake Formation, allow organizations to centralize and manage diverse data sources.

Example:

A financial institution using AI for fraud detection can store transactional data in a cloud data lake. The scalable storage allows for the retention of historical data, improving the accuracy of fraud models over time.

5.  **Containerization and Orchestration**

Overview:

Containerization encapsulates applications and their dependencies, ensuring consistency across different environments. Orchestration tools manage the deployment, scaling, and operation of containerized applications.

Implementation:

Docker is a popular containerization tool, and Kubernetes is widely used for orchestration. Together, they provide a scalable and portable solution for deploying AI applications in the cloud.

Example:

An ecommerce platform employing recommendation algorithms can use containerization and orchestration to deploy updated recommendation models seamlessly, ensuring a smooth user experience during high-traffic periods.

# Advanced Techniques in Cloud-Based Scalable AI

1.  **Distributed Deep Learning**

Overview:

Distributed deep learning involves training neural networks across multiple nodes or GPUs, reducing training time and enabling the processing of massive datasets.

Implementation:

Frameworks like TensorFlow and PyTorch support distributed training in the cloud. Services like AWS Deep Learning Containers provide preconfigured environments for distributed deep learning.

Example:

A company developing a computer vision model for autonomous vehicles can leverage distributed deep learning to train the model on a large dataset efficiently, speeding up the development process.

2. **Reinforcement Learning in the Cloud**

Overview:

Reinforcement learning involves training models through trial and error, and the cloud provides the necessary infrastructure to handle the computational demands of reinforcement learning algorithms.

Implementation:

Cloud-based services like Azure Machine Learning or Google AI Platform offer scalable environments for training and deploying reinforcement learning models. OpenAI's Gym toolkit can be integrated for environment simulations.

Example:

An online gaming platform can use reinforcement learning in the cloud to continuously optimize game environments and personalize user experiences based on individual player behaviors.

3. **Quantum Computing Integration**

Overview:

Quantum computing is on the horizon for cloud services, and its integration can potentially revolutionize AI computations, especially for complex tasks like optimization and machine learning.

Implementation:

While quantum computing for AI is still in the early stages, cloud providers like IBM and Rigetti offer access to quantum processing units. Integrating quantum computing into AI workflows may become more commonplace as the technology matures.

Example:

A pharmaceutical company aiming to discover new drug compounds can use quantum computing in the cloud to explore vast chemical spaces and identify potential candidates more efficiently than classical methods.

4. **AI Model Versioning and Deployment Pipelines**

Overview:

Versioning and systematically deploying AI models is crucial for maintaining consistency and ensuring that the latest models are in production.

Implementation:

Tools like MLflow or Kubeflow provide capabilities for managing model versions and deploying models in the cloud. Continuous integration and deployment (CI/CD) pipelines streamline the process.

Example:

An ecommerce platform using a recommendation system can use model versioning to seamlessly roll out updates, ensuring that users receive personalized recommendations based on the latest models.

5. **Transfer Learning at Scale**

Overview:

Transfer learning involves using pretrained models as a starting point for new tasks, reducing the amount of training data and computational resources required.

Implementation:

Cloud platforms offer pretrained models and specialized services for transfer learning. For example, Google Cloud's AutoML Vision allows developers to leverage pretrained models for image recognition tasks.

Example:

A healthcare application aiming to identify rare medical conditions from X-ray images can use transfer learning to start with a pretrained model on general medical images and fine-tune it for specific conditions, saving time and resources.

6. **Edge AI and Cloud Integration**

Overview:

Edge AI involves processing data locally on devices rather than relying solely on cloud servers. Integrating edge and cloud computing optimizes resource usage and response times.

Implementation:

Cloud providers offer services that seamlessly integrate edge devices with cloud resources. Azure IoT Edge, for instance, allows AI models to run on edge devices while connecting to Azure for additional processing and analytics.

Example:

A smart home security system can use edge AI for immediate facial recognition at the doorbell, while the cloud processes historical data and performs advanced analytics for improved security.

# Real-World Use Cases

1. **Netflix: Recommendation Systems at Scale**

   Overview:

   Netflix employs scalable AI to provide personalized recommendations to its millions of users, enhancing user satisfaction and retention.

   Implementation:

   Netflix utilizes a combination of distributed computing, containerization, and machine learning to process massive amounts of viewer data. The recommendation models are deployed in a scalable cloud environment to handle varying user loads.

   Example:

   As a user watches shows and movies on Netflix, the recommendation system continuously adapts, suggesting new content based on viewing history, preferences, and global trends.

2. **Google Photos: Image Recognition at Scale**

   Overview:

   Google Photos leverages scalable AI to provide users with features like automatic image categorization and facial recognition.

   Implementation:

   Distributed deep learning is used to train models that can recognize objects and faces within images. The cloud infrastructure ensures that image processing can scale to accommodate the vast number of photos uploaded daily.

   Example:

   When a user searches for "beach" in Google Photos, the scalable AI system quickly retrieves relevant images, showcasing the power of distributed deep learning in image recognition.

3.  **Uber: Dynamic Pricing with Machine Learning**

    Overview:

    Uber utilizes machine learning for dynamic pricing, adjusting ride costs based on real-time demand and supply factors.

    Implementation:

    Uber's pricing algorithm relies on machine learning models deployed in the cloud. These models consider factors like historical ride data, time of day, and local events to determine optimal pricing.

    Example:

    During a concert or sporting event, the demand for rides increases. Uber's dynamic pricing model, backed by scalable cloud infrastructure, adjusts prices to balance supply and demand, optimizing earnings for drivers.

4.  **Amazon Web Services (AWS): SageMaker for End-to-End ML Workflow**

    Overview:

    AWS SageMaker is a fully managed service that covers the entire machine learning workflow, from data labeling and model training to deployment and monitoring.

    Implementation:

    SageMaker simplifies the deployment of machine learning models at scale. It includes features for automated model training, deployment with one-click scaling, and monitoring model performance.

    Example:

    A financial institution using SageMaker can streamline the development of fraud detection models. The platform's scalability ensures that the model adapts to evolving fraud patterns and can handle large transaction volumes.

Advancements in cloud computing for scalable AI have transformed the landscape of artificial intelligence, providing a robust foundation for organizations to harness the power of machine learning and deep learning at scale. From elastic auto-scaling to cutting-edge techniques like distributed deep learning and quantum computing integration, the cloud offers a dynamic environment for deploying and managing advanced AI systems.

As we look to the future, trends like hybrid and multi-cloud environments, AI model marketplaces, and automated machine learning promise to further democratize AI development and optimize resource utilization. By addressing challenges related to cost management, data security, and model explainability, organizations can unlock the full potential of cloud-based scalable AI, driving innovation and enhancing decision-making across various industries.

# Edge Computing and AI Integration: Practices, Strategies, and Advanced Techniques for Scalable Systems

Edge computing, in conjunction with artificial intelligence (AI), has emerged as a transformative force in the world of technology. This integration brings computing power closer to data sources, enabling real-time processing and enhancing the scalability of AI systems. In this detailed exploration, we will delve into the practices and strategies that underpin the seamless integration of edge computing and AI, with a focus on supporting scalable systems. Additionally, advanced techniques, use cases, and examples will be provided to illustrate the practical implications of this powerful combination.

Edge computing involves processing data closer to the source of generation rather than relying solely on centralized cloud servers. This approach reduces latency, and bandwidth usage, and enhances the ability to process data in real time.

Integrating AI into edge computing involves deploying machine learning models and algorithms directly on edge devices or local servers. This enables intelligent decision-making at the edge, without the need for constant communication with a centralized cloud.

# Practices for Seamless Integration

1. **Optimized Model Deployment**

   Strategy:

   To support scalable AI systems, deploy lightweight and optimized machine learning models at the edge. These models should strike a balance between accuracy and computational efficiency.

   Advanced technique:

   Use quantization techniques to reduce the precision of model parameters, making them more suitable for deployment on edge devices with limited computational resources.

   Example:

   Consider an image recognition model deployed on a surveillance camera at the edge. By optimizing the model through quantization, the camera can efficiently analyze video feeds, identifying objects in real time.

2. **Decentralized Data Processing**

   Strategy:

   Distribute data processing tasks across edge devices to prevent bottlenecks and enhance overall system efficiency. Each edge device processes relevant data locally, reducing the need for centralized processing.

   Advanced technique:
   Implement a decentralized consensus algorithm to coordinate data processing tasks among edge devices, ensuring synchronization and avoiding conflicts.

   Example:

   In a smart city deployment, edge devices in different locations process local sensor data independently, and the consensus algorithm ensures that the overall system maintains a unified and accurate representation of the city's status.

3.  **Dynamic Resource Allocation**

    Strategy:

    Enable dynamic allocation of computing resources based on the varying demands of AI workloads. This ensures that edge devices efficiently utilize available resources while adapting to changing computational requirements.

    Advanced technique:

    Implement reinforcement learning algorithms for dynamic resource allocation, allowing edge devices to autonomously adjust resources based on historical usage patterns.

    Example:

    In an industrial setting, edge devices equipped with reinforcement learning can optimize the allocation of resources for predictive maintenance tasks, ensuring that critical machinery is monitored with minimal latency.

4.  **Federated Learning at the Edge**

    Strategy:

    Implement federated learning to train machine learning models across distributed edge devices. This approach allows models to learn from local data without compromising user privacy.

    Advanced technique:

    Incorporate differential privacy techniques into federated learning to further enhance privacy protection, ensuring that individual data contributions remain confidential.

    Example:

    In a healthcare application, federated learning at the edge allows models to be trained on patient data from various devices without centralizing sensitive information. Differential privacy ensures that individual patient data remains confidential.

# Use Cases: Real-World Applications of Edge Computing and AI Integration

1. **Autonomous Vehicles**

   Scenario:

   Edge computing and AI integration play a crucial role in the functioning of autonomous vehicles. Onboard sensors generate massive amounts of data that require real-time processing for decision-making.

   Implementation:

   Edge devices within the vehicle process sensor data locally, making instant decisions regarding navigation, obstacle avoidance, and traffic interactions. Federated learning is employed to continuously improve the vehicle's AI model based on collective experiences across a fleet of autonomous vehicles.

2. **Smart Retail**

   Scenario:

   In smart retail environments, the integration of edge computing and AI enhances customer experiences and optimizes operations. Edge devices at the store level process data from cameras, sensors, and customer interactions.

   Implementation:

   Local processing enables real-time analysis of customer behavior, allowing for personalized recommendations and targeted advertising. Dynamic resource allocation ensures that computing resources are allocated efficiently during peak shopping hours.

3. **Healthcare Monitoring**

   Scenario:

   Edge computing and AI are instrumental in remote healthcare monitoring, where continuous data streams from wearable devices and sensors need to be analyzed in real time.

217

Implementation:

Edge devices process health data locally, monitoring vital signs and identifying potential health issues. Federated learning ensures that machine learning models for health predictions improve over time without compromising the privacy of individual patients.

# Advanced Techniques in Code

1. **Optimized Model Deployment with TensorFlow Lite**

```python
import tensorflow as tf
from tensorflow import lite

 Load the pre-trained model
model = tf.keras.models.load_model('optimized_model.h5')

 Convert the model to TensorFlow Lite format
converter = lite.TFLiteConverter.from_keras_model(model)
tflite_model = converter.convert()

 Save the TensorFlow Lite model to a file
with open('optimized_model.tflite', 'wb') as f:
    f.write(tflite_model)
```

2. **Decentralized Data Processing with MQTT (Message Queuing Telemetry Transport)**

```python
import paho.mqtt.client as mqtt

 Define the callback function for message processing
def on_message(client, userdata, msg):
    Process the received message locally
    process_data(msg.payload)

 Set up the MQTT client
```

```python
client = mqtt.Client()
client.on_message = on_message
```

Connect to the MQTT broker
```python
client.connect("broker.example.com", 1883, 60)
```

Subscribe to a topic for data processing
```python
client.subscribe("edge/data")
```

Start the MQTT client loop for the continuous listening
```python
client.loop_start()
```
```

3. **Dynamic Resource Allocation with Reinforcement Learning in Python**

```python
import numpy as np
```

Define the state space, action space, and reward function
```python
state_space = [0, 1, 2, 3, 4]
action_space = [0, 1, 2]
rewards = np.array([[1, 0, -1],
                    [-1, 1, 0],
                    [0, -1, 1],
                    [1, 0, -1],
                    [-1, 1, 0]])
```

Q-learning algorithm for dynamic resource allocation
```python
def q_learning(state, alpha=0.1, gamma=0.9, epsilon=0.1, num_
episodes=1000):
    q_table = np.zeros((len(state_space), len(action_space)))

    for _ in range(num_episodes):
        current_state = np.random.choice(state_space)

        while True:
            if np.random.uniform(0, 1) < epsilon:
                action = np.random.choice(action_space)
            else:
```

219
```

```
            action = np.argmax(q_table[current_state, :])

        next_state = np.random.choice(state_space)
        reward = rewards[current_state, action]

        q_table[current_state, action] = (1 - alpha)
        * q_table[current_state, action] + \
                                    alpha * (reward +
                                    gamma * np.max
                                    (q_table[next_
                                    state, :]))

        current_state = next_state

        if current_state == len(state_space) - 1:
            break

    return q_table


  Example

  usage
q_table = q_learning(state_space)
print("Q-table:", q_table)
```
```

## 4.  **Federated Learning with PySyft (PyTorch)**

```python
import torch
import syft as sy

 Set up a PySyft hook for federated learning
hook = sy.TorchHook(torch)

 Define the local dataset
local_dataset = torch.randn((100, 10))

 Create a virtual worker representing the edge device
edge_device = sy.VirtualWorker(hook, id="edge_device")
```
```

```
Send the local dataset to the edge device
local_dataset_ptr = local_dataset.send(edge_device)

Define the model
model = torch.nn.Linear(10, 1)

Train the model using federated learning
for epoch in range(10):
    Perform local training on the edge device
    local_model = model.copy().send(edge_device)
    local_optimizer = torch.optim.SGD(params=local_model.
    parameters(), lr=0.01)
    local_optimizer.zero_grad()
    local_loss = ((local_model(local_dataset_ptr)
    - target)  2).sum()
    local_loss.backward()
    local_optimizer.step()

    Update the global model with the local model's gradients
    model.weight.data.set_(((model.weight.data + local_model.
    weight.grad).get()))
    model.bias.data.set_(((model.bias.data + local_model.bias.
    grad).get()))

    Move the updated model back to the local device
    model.get()

Retrieve the final global model
final_model = model.get()
```

The seamless integration of edge computing and AI presents a paradigm shift in the scalability and efficiency of intelligent systems. Practices such as optimized model deployment, decentralized data processing, dynamic resource allocation, and federated learning play pivotal roles in supporting scalable AI systems at the edge. Advanced techniques, illustrated through real-world use cases and code examples, showcase the practical implementation of these strategies. As technology continues to evolve, the synergy between edge computing and AI will undoubtedly drive innovations across diverse domains, from autonomous vehicles to healthcare, revolutionizing the way we interact with and benefit from intelligent systems.

# AI Hardware Innovations for Scalability

Artificial intelligence (AI) has become an integral part of various industries, driving innovation and efficiency. As the demand for AI applications grows, the need for scalable AI systems becomes paramount. Scalability ensures that AI models can handle increasing workloads without compromising performance. One crucial aspect of achieving scalability is the development of advanced AI hardware. In this comprehensive exploration, we delve into AI hardware innovations geared toward scalability. We'll discuss best practices, strategies, and cutting-edge techniques, supported by real-world examples and code snippets to provide a tangible understanding of these concepts.

Scalable AI systems are designed to adapt to the increasing demands of data processing and model complexity. Achieving scalability involves addressing challenges related to computation power, memory, and communication bandwidth. As we delve into AI hardware innovations, let's explore the practices and strategies that contribute to scalable AI systems.

1.  **Parallel Processing Architectures**
    Overview:
    Parallel processing involves breaking down a large task into smaller subtasks that can be processed simultaneously. This approach significantly speeds up computation, making it a key strategy for scalable AI systems.

    Practices:

    –   **Data Parallelism**: Distributing data across multiple processors to perform the same operation concurrently

    –   **Model Parallelism**: Dividing a neural network into segments and assigning each segment to a different processor

Example:

Consider a deep learning model. Data parallelism allows different processors to simultaneously process different batches of data during training, accelerating the overall training process.

Code snippet (TensorFlow):

```python
 Using TensorFlow's `tf.distribute.MirroredStrategy` for data
parallelism
strategy = tf.distribute.MirroredStrategy()

with strategy.scope():
    Define and compile the model here
   model = ...

    Model training code here
   model.fit(...)
```

2. **Specialized AI Accelerators**

Overview:

Specialized hardware accelerators, such as Graphics Processing Units (GPUs) and Tensor Processing Units (TPUs), are designed to handle AI workloads efficiently. These accelerators are optimized for the specific matrix operations prevalent in deep learning.

Practices:

- **Utilizing GPU Clusters**: Configuring multiple GPUs in a cluster to distribute workloads

- **Custom Hardware Accelerators**: Designing application-specific integrated circuits (ASICs) for AI tasks

Example:

In natural language processing, models like OpenAI's GPT-3 leverage GPU clusters to process vast amounts of text data efficiently, enabling sophisticated language understanding.

3. **Memory Optimization**

Overview:

Memory plays a crucial role in the performance of AI systems. Optimizing memory usage is essential for scalability, especially when dealing with large datasets and complex models.

Practices:

- **Memory Compression Techniques**: Reducing the memory footprint of model parameters

- **Data Streaming**: Loading and processing data in smaller chunks to minimize memory requirements.

Example:

In image recognition, memory optimization techniques enable the efficient processing of high-resolution images without overwhelming the system's memory.
Code snippet (PyTorch):

```python
 Using PyTorch's memory optimization techniques
torch.backends.cuda.memory_stats(device=None)
```

4. **Distributed Computing**

Overview:

Distributed computing involves spreading computations across multiple machines. This strategy enhances scalability by enabling the parallel processing of data on a larger scale.

Practices:

- **Data Parallelism Across Nodes**: Distributing data and computations across multiple servers

- **Message Passing Interface (MPI)**: Facilitating communication between distributed nodes

Example:

In training large-scale neural networks, distributed computing allows for the collaboration of multiple GPUs or even multiple machines, significantly reducing training times.
Code snippet (MPI in Python):

```python
 Using mpi4py for MPI communication
from mpi4py import MPI

comm = MPI.COMM_WORLD
rank = comm.Get_rank()

 MPI communication and computation code here
```

# Advanced Techniques for AI Hardware Innovations

As we explore practices and strategies, it's crucial to delve into advanced techniques that push the boundaries of AI hardware innovations. These techniques not only enhance scalability but also open new possibilities for AI applications:

1. **Quantum Computing for AI**

   Overview:

   Quantum computing leverages the principles of quantum mechanics to perform computations at speeds unattainable by classical computers. In the context of scalable AI, quantum computing holds the potential to revolutionize the training of large and intricate machine learning models.

   Practices:

   - **Quantum Circuit Simulation**: Implementing quantum circuits for specific AI tasks

   - **Quantum Machine Learning Algorithms**: Developing algorithms that harness the power of quantum computing for AI

225

Quantum Computing Hardware Preferences:

When considering hardware for running quantum computing programs, it's essential to focus on the unique requirements of quantum systems. Quantum computers use qubits, the quantum counterparts to classical bits, and operate on principles like superposition and entanglement. Key considerations for hardware include the following:

**Quantum Processing Units (QPUs)**: QPUs serve as the quantum equivalent of classical CPUs, essential for quantum computation. Examples include IBM Quantum processors, Google's Sycamore processor, and offerings from Rigetti and IonQ.

**Cryogenic Systems**: Due to the sensitivity of quantum states, quantum computers typically operate at extremely low temperatures, requiring specialized cryogenic systems.

**Control Electronics**: Essential electronics for controlling and reading qubits, involving components like microwave pulse generators and control lines.

**Quantum Error Correction**: Quantum computers employ specialized circuits and extra qubits for error correction, a crucial aspect due to the vulnerability of qubits to errors.

**Connectivity**: Quantum computers require advanced interconnects for effective communication between qubits, often involving superconducting circuits and waveguide networks.

Quantum Computing Frameworks and Libraries:

Frameworks and libraries play a pivotal role in simplifying quantum programming. They provide tools and abstractions, facilitating the development process. Popular quantum computing frameworks and libraries include

**Qiskit**: An open source quantum computing software development framework developed by IBM

**Cirq**: A Python library by Google designed for writing, simulating, and executing quantum circuits on Google's quantum processors

**QuTiP (Quantum Toolbox in Python)**: An open source Python library for simulating the dynamics of open quantum systems

**Forest (pyQuil)**: A suite of tools by Rigetti Computing, which includes pyQuil, a Python library for quantum programming

**ProjectQ**: An open source quantum software framework for quantum computing

These tools empower developers to work with quantum computers effectively, providing a range of functionalities from circuit design to simulation and execution.
Please note that the specifics of code implementation would depend on the chosen framework and the quantum hardware being utilized.

Example:

In optimization tasks like hyperparameter tuning, quantum computing can explore a vast solution space simultaneously, potentially finding optimal configurations faster than classical algorithms.

Code snippet (Qiskit for quantum computing in Python):

```python
 Using Qiskit for quantum circuit simulation
from qiskit import QuantumCircuit, transpile, assemble

qc = QuantumCircuit(3, 3)
 Quantum circuit construction code here

 Transpile the quantum circuit for a specific quantum processor
transpiled_circuit = transpile(qc, backend=...)

 Assemble the transpired circuit for execution
qobj = assemble(transpiled_circuit)
```

2. **Neuromorphic Computing Architectures**

Overview:

Neuromorphic computing mimics the structure and function
of the human brain. Rather than relying on traditional binary
logic, neuromorphic systems use artificial neurons to process
information, enabling more efficient and brain-like computation.

Practices:

- **Spiking Neural Networks**: Emulating the spiking behavior of neurons
  in the brain

- **Event-Driven Processing**: Processing information only when there is
  a change in input, reducing overall energy consumption

Example:

In robotics, neuromorphic computing allows for real-time,
energy-efficient processing, enabling robots to adapt to dynamic
environments with low power consumption.

3. **AI Hardware Codesign**

Overview:

AI hardware codesign involves developing hardware architectures
that are specifically tailored to the requirements of AI algorithms.
This collaborative approach between hardware and software
design ensures optimal performance.

Practices:

- **Custom Hardware for Neural Network Layers**: Designing hardware
  modules optimized for specific layers in a neural network

- **Dynamic Reconfigurability**: Allowing hardware to adapt dynamically
  to different AI workloads

Example:

In edge computing scenarios, AI hardware codesign enables
the creation of energy-efficient processors capable of running
complex models on resource-constrained devices.

Code snippet (Vivado HLS for FPGA codesign):

```c
// Using Vivado HLS for co-design on FPGA
pragma HLS INTERFACE s_axilite port=return bundle=CTRL
pragma HLS INTERFACE m_axi depth=256 port=input offset=slave
bundle=DATA
pragma HLS INTERFACE m_axi depth=256 port=output offset=slave
bundle=DATA

// HLS code for custom hardware acceleration here
```

# Use Cases and Real-World Examples

Understanding the theoretical aspects of AI hardware innovations is crucial, but real-world applications provide tangible proof of their impact. Let's explore several use cases and examples where these practices and strategies have been successfully applied:

1. **Google's Tensor Processing Units (TPUs)**

   Use case:

   Google's TPUs are custom-designed AI accelerators optimized for machine learning workloads. These TPUs have been instrumental in accelerating the training and inference of deep learning models on Google Cloud.

   Example:

   In natural language processing, models like BERT have seen significant speedup in training times when utilizing Google TPUs, allowing for more rapid experimentation and development of advanced language models.

2. **IBM Quantum Computers for Machine Learning**

   Use case:

   IBM's quantum computers, available through the IBM Quantum Experience platform, provide researchers and developers with access to quantum computing resources. This opens up new avenues for exploring quantum algorithms for machine learning tasks.

Example:

Quantum machine learning algorithms, such as Quantum Support Vector Machines, have been implemented on IBM's quantum computers, showcasing the potential of quantum computing for enhancing classical machine learning tasks.

3. **SpiNNaker Neuromorphic Supercomputer**

   Use case:

   The SpiNNaker (Spiking Neural Network Architecture) supercomputer is designed to simulate the human brain's spiking neural networks. It is employed in various neuroscience and AI research projects.

   Example:

   In cognitive robotics, SpiNNaker has been used to simulate large-scale neural networks, allowing researchers to study and understand the principles of brain-inspired computing.

# Implications for the Future

AI hardware innovations for scalability hold immense potential, but their adoption comes with certain implications and considerations:

1. **Evolving Skillsets**

   As AI hardware evolves, there is a growing need for professionals with expertise in both hardware and software. Skillsets encompassing hardware design, algorithm development, and system optimization will be increasingly valuable.

2. **Energy Efficiency**

   While AI hardware innovations strive for greater performance,
   energy efficiency is a critical factor. Balancing computational
   power with energy consumption becomes imperative, especially
   in scenarios where resources are constrained.

3. **Interdisciplinary Collaboration**

   AI hardware innovations necessitate collaboration between
   hardware engineers, software developers, and domain experts.
   Interdisciplinary teams will drive the codesign of hardware and
   algorithms for optimal performance.

4. **Ethical Considerations**

   As AI becomes more integrated into society, ethical considerations
   regarding data privacy, bias, and responsible AI development
   become even more crucial. Hardware innovations must align with
   ethical principles to ensure fair and unbiased AI systems.

AI hardware innovations for scalability are at the forefront of advancing the
capabilities of artificial intelligence. From parallel processing architectures to quantum
computing and neuromorphic designs, these innovations pave the way for more
efficient, powerful, and adaptable AI systems. Real-world examples and code snippets
provide a tangible understanding of these concepts, emphasizing their practical
applications.

The future holds exciting possibilities as AI hardware continues to evolve,
driving breakthroughs in fields ranging from healthcare to robotics. Embracing these
innovations requires a holistic approach, considering not only technical advancements
but also ethical considerations and interdisciplinary collaboration. As we navigate
the complexities of scalable AI hardware, we unlock the potential to address grand
challenges and usher in a new era of intelligent computing.

# CHAPTER 12

# Conclusion and Final Thoughts

In the exploration of scalable AI systems throughout this book, we have traversed a comprehensive journey encompassing foundational concepts, advanced techniques, and real-world applications. As we conclude, let's recap the key takeaways from each chapter and reflect on the overarching themes.

Chapter 1: Introduction to Scalable AI Systems

Key Takeaways:

- Scalable AI systems are vital for handling increasing workloads and building robust intelligent solutions.

- Design patterns play a crucial role in ensuring the resilience and efficiency of scalable AI architectures.

- Challenges and considerations in scalable AI systems highlight the importance of a holistic approach to system design.

Chapter 2: Fundamentals of Scalability in AI

Key Takeaways:

- Handling large datasets requires scalable solutions for efficient storage and retrieval.

- Distributed computing and parallel processing techniques are fundamental for achieving scalability.

- Scaling AI models involves optimizing algorithms and infrastructure to meet growing computational demands.

© Abhishek Mishra 2024
A. Mishra, *Scalable AI and Design Patterns*, https://doi.org/10.1007/979-8-8688-0158-7_12

Chapter 3: Data Engineering for Scalable AI

Key Takeaways:

- Effective data engineering practices are essential for supporting scalable AI systems.

- Data ingestion, preprocessing, and feature engineering at scale are critical components of the data engineering process.

- Strategic data storage and management are foundational for scalable AI solutions.

Chapter 4: Scalable AI Algorithms and Models

Key Takeaways:

- Distributed training, online learning, and model parallelism are key techniques for handling large-scale data and computing requirements.

- Scalable AI models require sophisticated algorithms that can adapt to dynamic workloads.

Chapter 5: Scalable AI Infrastructure and Architecture

Key Takeaways:

- Containerization, orchestration, and resource management are pivotal for creating scalable AI infrastructure.

- Auto-scaling strategies enable systems to adapt to varying workloads efficiently.

Chapter 6: Scalable AI Deployment and Productionization

Key Takeaways:

- Model versioning, deployment strategies, and monitoring are crucial for successful deployment.

- Building production-grade AI systems involves optimizing performance and ensuring reliability.

Chapter 7: Scalable AI for Real-Time and Streaming Data

Key Takeaways:

– Scalable AI systems for real-time and streaming data require specialized techniques for handling high-velocity data.

– Real-time inference techniques are vital for applications demanding instant responses.

Chapter 8: Scalable AI for Edge Computing

Key Takeaways:

– Edge device architectures must be designed to accommodate the unique constraints of edge computing environments.

– Edge AI model optimization and integration with cloud services enhance scalability in edge scenarios.

Chapter 9: Scalable AI Governance and Ethics

Key Takeaways:

– Mitigating bias, ensuring fairness, and prioritizing interpretability are critical for ethical AI development.

– Privacy considerations are paramount in scalable AI systems to uphold user trust.

Chapter 10: Case Studies and Best Practices

Key Takeaways:

– Real-world case studies provide insights into successful implementations of scalable AI solutions.

– Best practices emphasize the importance of thoughtful design and implementation for scalable AI systems.

Chapter 11: Future Trends and Emerging Technologies

Key Takeaways:

– Advancements in cloud computing, integration of edge computing, and AI hardware innovations are shaping the future of scalable AI.

# Final Thoughts

In closing, the exploration of scalable AI systems has been a dynamic and enlightening journey. The convergence of foundational principles, innovative techniques, and ethical considerations underscores the complexity of building intelligent systems capable of adapting to the evolving demands of the AI landscape.

As we look to the future, the integration of cloud and edge computing, coupled with AI hardware innovations, promises unprecedented scalability and efficiency. However, it is crucial to navigate these advancements with a mindful consideration of ethical implications, governance, and user privacy.

# Key Takeaways from the Book

1. **Scalable AI Is Fundamental**: Scalable AI systems are indispensable for meeting the growing demands of data processing and model complexity.

2. **Design Patterns Matter**: Design patterns play a pivotal role in building robust and scalable intelligent solutions.

3. **Data Engineering Is the Backbone**: Effective data engineering practices, from ingestion to storage, form the backbone of scalable AI systems.

4. **Algorithmic Innovation Is Key**: Scalable AI models require innovative algorithms, with distributed training and model parallelism at the forefront.

5. **Infrastructure Matters**: Thoughtful infrastructure design, including containerization, orchestration, and resource management, is crucial for scalability.

6. **Deployment Is Not the End**: Successful deployment involves versioning, monitoring, and continuous optimization for production-grade AI systems.

7. **Real-Time and Edge Are the Future**: Scalable AI must adapt to real-time and edge computing scenarios, necessitating specialized techniques and architectures.

8. **Ethics Cannot Be Overlooked**: Governance, fairness, interpretability, and privacy considerations are integral to ethical scalable AI development.

9. **Learn from the Best**: Real-world case studies and best practices provide valuable insights for designing and implementing scalable AI systems.

10. **Future Trends Shape the Landscape**: Cloud computing advancements, edge computing integration, and AI hardware innovations are key drivers of future scalability.

In embracing these takeaways, we equip ourselves to navigate the evolving landscape of scalable AI, ensuring that our intelligent systems not only meet the demands of today but also anticipate and adapt to the challenges of tomorrow.

# The Significance of Scalable AI in Shaping the Future

The burgeoning landscape of artificial intelligence (AI) is continually evolving, and within this dynamic environment, the importance of scalable AI stands as a cornerstone for the future. Scalability in AI systems is not merely a technological feature but a strategic imperative that underpins the development, deployment, and sustainability of intelligent solutions. In this comprehensive exploration, we delve into the multifaceted dimensions of the importance of scalable AI, exploring its implications across various sectors, technological advancements, and ethical considerations. From its foundational role in meeting escalating computational demands to its pivotal role in fostering innovation, scalable AI emerges as a transformative force shaping the trajectory of AI technologies in the years to come.

# I. Foundational Pillars of Scalable AI

1.  Meeting Growing Demands

    As the volume and complexity of data continue to surge,
    scalable AI systems are indispensable for meeting the escalating
    demands of data processing and analysis. Traditional computing
    architectures often struggle to cope with the sheer magnitude of
    data generated in diverse fields, from healthcare and finance to
    manufacturing and entertainment. Scalable AI, with its ability
    to efficiently scale computational resources, emerges as the
    linchpin for handling the immense datasets characteristic of the
    modern era.

2.  Adapting to Dynamic Workloads

    In dynamic environments where workloads fluctuate, the
    adaptability of scalable AI systems becomes a strategic advantage.
    Whether it's the ecommerce sector handling peak shopping
    seasons or cloud-based platforms managing varying user
    demands, scalable AI ensures that computational resources can
    be dynamically allocated and scaled, optimizing efficiency and
    performance.

3.  Facilitating Rapid Prototyping and Experimentation

    Scalable AI's significance extends beyond addressing
    computational challenges; it is a catalyst for innovation. In
    research and development, the ability to rapidly prototype and
    experiment with diverse AI models is paramount. Scalable
    systems empower researchers and data scientists to iterate
    through models efficiently, fostering a culture of experimentation
    that is fundamental for pushing the boundaries of AI capabilities.

# II. Scalable AI Across Industries

1.  Healthcare Revolution

    In the healthcare sector, the importance of scalable AI is vividly
    evident in its potential to revolutionize diagnostics, drug
    discovery, and patient care. With the exponential growth of
    medical data, scalable AI becomes the linchpin for developing
    predictive models, optimizing treatment plans, and accelerating
    the pace of medical research. The ability to scale computational
    resources in healthcare settings translates to quicker analyses,
    leading to timely and accurate diagnoses.

2.  Financial Sector Innovation

    The financial sector is another arena where scalable AI plays a pivotal
    role. From algorithmic trading to fraud detection and risk management,
    the financial industry relies on scalable AI systems to process vast
    datasets in real time. Scalable AI algorithms can analyze market trends,
    identify anomalies, and adapt to changing financial landscapes,
    providing a competitive edge and enhancing decision-making processes.

3.  Manufacturing Efficiency

    In manufacturing, scalability is instrumental in enhancing
    efficiency and optimizing production processes. Scalable AI
    systems can analyze production data, predict equipment failures,
    and automate quality control processes. The adaptability of
    scalable AI allows manufacturers to scale their AI applications as
    production demands fluctuate, ensuring seamless integration into
    dynamic manufacturing environments.

4.  Entertainment and Content Creation
    The entertainment industry is experiencing a paradigm shift driven
    by scalable AI. Content recommendation algorithms, video streaming
    optimization, and personalized user experiences rely on scalable AI
    systems to process and analyze user data at scale. Scalable AI not only
    ensures a seamless user experience but also facilitates the creation of
    tailored content that resonates with diverse audiences.

# III. Technological Advancements and Scalable AI

1.  Advancements in Cloud Computing

    The evolution of cloud computing is intricately linked with
    the importance of scalable AI. Cloud platforms provide the
    infrastructure and resources needed for scalable AI applications
    to thrive. Scalable AI algorithms, when deployed in cloud
    environments, can dynamically scale based on demand, enabling
    cost-effective and efficient utilization of computational resources.
    This symbiotic relationship between scalable AI and cloud
    computing lays the foundation for the next era of intelligent
    systems.

2.  Edge Computing Integration

    As the Internet of Things (IoT) expands, the integration of scalable
    AI with edge computing becomes imperative. Edge devices, with
    their constrained resources, benefit immensely from scalable
    AI architectures that can optimize model size and adapt to the
    limited computational capabilities of edge devices. Scalable AI
    for edge computing ensures that intelligent decision-making
    processes occur at the source of data generation, reducing latency
    and enhancing responsiveness.

3.  AI Hardware Innovations

    The emergence of specialized AI hardware, such as Graphics
    Processing Units (GPUs) and Tensor Processing Units (TPUs),
    underscores the importance of scalable AI. These hardware
    innovations are designed to handle the intensive computational
    requirements of AI workloads. Scalable AI leverages these
    advancements, ensuring that models can scale across diverse
    hardware architectures, from traditional CPUs to specialized AI
    accelerators.

# IV. Ethical Considerations in Scalable AI

1. Bias Mitigation and Fairness

   Ethical considerations in AI are magnified in scalable systems.
   The importance of mitigating bias and ensuring fairness becomes
   paramount, especially as scalable AI systems are deployed across
   diverse demographics and industries. Without ethical safeguards,
   scalable AI could inadvertently perpetuate and amplify biases
   present in training data, leading to unfair outcomes.

2. Interpretability and Explainability

   Scalable AI systems often involve complex models and algorithms.
   The challenge of ensuring interpretability and explainability
   becomes more pronounced in scalable architectures. Ethical AI
   development necessitates transparency, allowing stakeholders to
   understand how decisions are made. Scalable AI solutions must
   incorporate methods for making the decision-making process
   interpretable, especially in critical applications like healthcare
   and finance.

3. Privacy in the Era of Scalability

   As AI systems scale to process massive datasets, privacy
   considerations become paramount. Scalable AI must incorporate
   robust privacy-preserving techniques to safeguard sensitive
   information. An ethical approach to scalability involves adopting
   encryption, anonymization, and other privacy-enhancing
   technologies to ensure that individual privacy rights are protected.

# V. The Future Landscape: Scalable AI's Role

1. Advancements in Cloud Computing for Scalable AI

   The future of scalable AI is intricately linked to advancements
   in cloud computing. Cloud platforms will continue to evolve,
   offering more sophisticated tools and services that seamlessly

integrate with scalable AI architectures. This synergy will democratize access to scalable AI, empowering organizations of all sizes to harness the benefits of intelligent and scalable systems.

2. Edge Computing and AI Integration

The integration of edge computing with scalable AI will witness exponential growth. Edge devices will become more intelligent and capable of processing and analyzing data locally with the support of scalable AI architectures. This distributed intelligence at the edge will usher in a new era of real-time decision-making, with applications ranging from autonomous vehicles to smart cities.

3. AI Hardware Innovations for Scalability

The future will witness continuous innovations in AI hardware, further enhancing the scalability of AI systems. Quantum computing, neuromorphic architectures, and customized AI accelerators will redefine the boundaries of what is achievable in terms of scalability. As hardware becomes more specialized and efficient, scalable AI will harness these advancements to push the limits of computational capabilities.

The significance of scalable AI in shaping the future is profound and multifaceted. From its foundational role in meeting computational demands to its transformative impact across industries and its synergy with technological advancements, scalable AI emerges as a linchpin for the future of artificial intelligence. As we navigate this landscape, it is imperative to recognize the ethical considerations inherent in scalable AI and to envision a future where intelligent systems prioritize fairness, interpretability, and privacy.

Scalable AI is not merely a technological tool; it is a paradigm shift that empowers organizations and individuals to navigate the complexities of the digital age. The future promises seamless integration of scalable AI with advancements in cloud computing, edge computing, and AI hardware innovations, ushering in an era where intelligent systems adapt, innovate, and contribute to the betterment of society. As we embrace the future, the importance of scalable AI remains at the forefront, shaping the trajectory of AI technologies and influencing the way we interact with, benefit from, and trust intelligent systems.

# Final Reflections on Design Patterns for Robust Intelligent Systems

As we conclude our exploration into the realm of design patterns for robust intelligent systems, it is essential to reflect on the profound impact these patterns have on the development, deployment, and sustainability of advanced AI solutions. Design patterns serve as architectural blueprints, guiding developers in crafting resilient, scalable, and efficient intelligent systems. In this final reflection, we delve into the key insights gained from our journey through the intricate landscape of design patterns, emphasizing their pivotal role in ensuring the robustness and reliability of intelligent systems.

## I. Design Patterns As Building Blocks

1. Architectural Foundations

   Design patterns lay the architectural foundations for intelligent systems, providing a structured and standardized approach to problem-solving. Whether addressing issues of scalability, adaptability, or maintainability, these patterns serve as building blocks that imbue systems with the flexibility to evolve and meet the dynamic demands of an ever-changing technological landscape.

2. Flexibility and Adaptability

   One of the salient features of design patterns is their inherent flexibility. By encapsulating best practices and proven solutions, these patterns empower developers to adapt and extend their designs based on specific requirements. This adaptability is crucial in the context of intelligent systems, where the ability to accommodate evolving datasets, changing user needs, and emerging technologies is paramount.

# II. Enhancing Robustness Through Design Patterns

1.   Resilience to Change

     Intelligent systems are not static entities; they must evolve to
     remain relevant. Design patterns provide a framework for creating
     systems that are resilient to change. Whether it's incorporating
     new features, accommodating shifting user expectations, or
     integrating advancements in AI algorithms, design patterns
     ensure that the underlying architecture can seamlessly adapt
     without compromising robustness.

2.   Scalability and Performance Optimization

     Scalability is a central concern in the realm of intelligent systems.
     Design patterns tailored for scalability ensure that systems can
     efficiently handle growing datasets and increasing computational
     demands. Patterns such as the Observer, Strategy, and Command
     patterns, when applied judiciously, contribute to the optimization
     of system performance, enabling the seamless execution of
     complex AI algorithms.

# III. Maintenance and Sustainability

1.   Maintainability Through Modularity

     The longevity of intelligent systems is intricately tied to their
     maintainability. Design patterns promote modularity, dividing
     complex systems into manageable and independent components.
     This modularity facilitates easier maintenance, debugging, and
     updates, ensuring that intelligent systems can be sustained over
     time with minimal disruptions.

2.   Documentation and Knowledge Transfer

     Design patterns act as a form of documentation, conveying best
     practices and architectural decisions. This documentation is
     invaluable for knowledge transfer within development teams.
     As team members change or new developers join a project, the

consistent application of design patterns aids in understanding the system's architecture, fostering a collaborative environment that is conducive to sustainable development.

# IV. Addressing Common Challenges

1. Handling Complexity

   Intelligent systems often grapple with inherent complexity arising from intricate algorithms, diverse data sources, and multifaceted user interactions. Design patterns offer systematic approaches to managing this complexity, providing abstraction layers that simplify interactions and encapsulate intricate functionalities. The Observer pattern, for example, elegantly addresses the challenge of handling complex event-driven architectures.

2. Ensuring Security and Privacy

   Security and privacy are nonnegotiable aspects of intelligent systems. Design patterns contribute to these concerns by offering templates for secure and privacy-preserving architectures. For instance, the Decorator pattern can be employed to dynamically add security layers to components, and the Proxy pattern can control access to sensitive data, ensuring robust security measures.

# V. Human-Centric Design Patterns

1. User Experience and Interface Design

   The user experience is at the forefront of intelligent system design. Design patterns extend beyond architectural considerations to encompass user interface and experience design. Patterns like the Observer and Strategy patterns are instrumental in creating responsive and intuitive interfaces, enhancing the overall usability of intelligent systems.

2.  Ethical Considerations in Design

    As intelligent systems become more integrated into everyday life,
    ethical considerations become paramount. Design patterns can
    play a role in promoting ethical practices. Patterns such as the
    Chain of Responsibility can be employed to incorporate ethical
    decision-making processes, ensuring that intelligent systems
    prioritize fairness, accountability, and transparency.

# VI. Continuous Learning and Evolution

1.  Adopting Emerging Technologies

    Design patterns are not static entities; they evolve alongside
    technological advancements. Staying attuned to emerging
    technologies and incorporating novel patterns allows intelligent
    systems to harness the latest innovations. For example, the
    adoption of patterns aligned with edge computing or quantum
    computing reflects the commitment to staying on the cutting edge
    of technological progress.

2.  Iterative Design and Feedback Loops

    The iterative nature of intelligent system development aligns
    seamlessly with design patterns. Continuous refinement based on
    user feedback and evolving requirements is facilitated by design
    patterns that support iterative design processes. The Observer
    pattern, in particular, aids in establishing effective feedback loops,
    ensuring that intelligent systems remain responsive to user needs.

In our final reflections on design patterns for robust intelligent systems, it becomes
evident that these patterns are not mere architectural elements; they are guiding
principles that influence the very essence of intelligent system development. From
foundational building blocks to addressing complex challenges, design patterns
serve as a compass, directing developers toward creating systems that are not only
technologically sophisticated but also resilient, adaptable, and ethically sound.

# Bibliography

https://arxiv.org/pdf/2304.11090 – A comprehensive review of design patterns for AI systems, categorized by architecture, deployment, implementation, and security

https://dzone.com/articles/scalable-system-design – Focuses on general, non-AI-specific design patterns applicable to building scalable systems

www.researchgate.net/publication/370464888_Design_Development_and_Implementation_of_Artificial_Intelligence_Technology_A_Scoping_Review – Explores the potential of applying software design patterns to AI system development

www.infoq.com/scalability/ – Provides an overview of common scalability patterns, including load balancing, caching, and distributed processing

https://medium.com/@i.vikas/the-intersection-of-system-design-and-ai-building-scalable-and-intelligent-systems-5784ca172ad2 – Discusses the intersection of system design and AI, highlighting relevant architectures and deployment strategies

These resources offer a deeper understanding of scalable AI design patterns and architectures. Remember, the best approach depends on your specific AI application and its unique requirements.

# Index

© Abhishek Mishra 2024
A. Mishra, *Scalable AI and Design Patterns*, https://doi.org/10.1007/979-8-8688-0158-7

Printed in the United States
by Baker & Taylor Publisher Services